NATIVE
AMERICAN
TRADITIONS

THE
ELEMENT
LIBRARY

NATIVE AMERICAN TRADITIONS

ARTHUR VERSLUIS

ELEMENT
Shaftesbury, Dorset
Rockport, Massachusetts
Brisbane, Queensland

© Element Books Limited 1994
Text © Arthur Versluis 1994

Published in Great Britain in 1994 by
ELEMENT BOOKS LIMITED
SHAFTESBURY, DORSET

Published in the USA in 1994 by
Element, Inc.
42 Broadway, Rockport, MA 01966

Published in Australia in 1994 by
Element Books Limited for
Jacaranda Wiley Limited
33 Park Road, Milton, Brisbane, 4064

ISBN 1-85230-572-X

Designed and typeset by
THE BRIDGEWATER BOOK COMPANY
Art Director *Annie Moss*
Designer *James Lawrence*
Managing Editor *Anna Clarkson*
Editors *Viv Croot, Carol McKendrick*
Picture researcher *Vanessa Fletcher*

Printed and bound in Great Britain

British Library Cataloguing-in-Publication Data available

Library of Congress Cataloging-in-Publication
Data available

CONTENTS

1

INTRODUCTION

Big Springs offers prayers to the sun. The sun was central to the Native American pantheon and was worshipped and celebrated in many different ways throughout the vast continent.

That the Native American religious traditions – with all their diversity – represent one of the world religions in the same way as does Hinduism, for instance, is a relatively recent concept in the Judaeo-Christian world. For centuries, Europeans, and European Americans, viewed the American Indian peoples with a combination of condescension, fascination, and, all too often, contempt and incomprehension. Only in the last few decades of the twentieth century has European American scholarship really begun to take a more open view of American Indian traditions, and only since then has a new view, which looks to the Native Americans for spiritual understanding, begun to appear more widely in 'mainstream' American society. Still there is much prejudice in America against American Indians; but as the destructiveness of the modern worldview has become more apparent, many people have turned to Native Americans to understand how better to live in harmony with the natural and spiritual realms. This book represents an introduction to that way.

The Native American tragedy

Of course, to study the history of European and European American relations to the American Indians is, for the most part, to view a tragedy. One sees there, a relationship that could have been fruitful, become instead a lesson in mutual incomprehension, not to mention greed and deceit on the part of many European Americans. If the white Americans found it difficult to conceive of nature as theophany in the Indian way, Native Americans, for their part, did not think in European terms of owning square sections of land. For Indian peoples, one's word was one's bond; if verbal assent was given by a council of leaders, then everyone would follow that agreement. Hence the failure of many whites to adhere even to written contracts, was particularly incomprehensible to tribal peoples, and all of this contributed to the countless tragedies of North and South American history.

In part, too, the tragedy of the Native American peoples reflects how they were simply overwhelmed by sheer population. Many of the Indian tribes were decimated or even obliterated by unfamiliar European diseases (sometimes deliberately introduced among them), by slaughter, by dispossession and by exhaustion of traditional game. Whites, however, flourished and moved inexorably westwards, taking over even lands contractually deeded to various tribes or confederacies. In the face of such obstacles, including the relentless erosion of traditional ways, and even by the outlawing of native religions, one is surprised that the Indian peoples have survived and preserved as much of their culture as they have.

Yet much has disappeared. When Europeans first landed on North and South American shores, the native traditions were extraordinarily diverse: ranging from the urban centres of the South American peoples to the nomadic traditions of the far north, from the Pueblo and Hopi traditions of the south-west, for instance, to the totemic traditions of the Pacific north-west. Both linguistically and culturally, the Native Americans were so diverse that one can hardly speak of a single American Indian religion. But much of this diversity has been lost, not least through the erosiveness of European-derived American civilization, and today one finds that many tribes follow similar patterns in meeting, in what Joseph Epes Brown has called the 'pow-wow syndrome'.

Sioux leaders gathered in Washington DC in 1875 to protest at the violation of the Fort Laramie Treaty, signed in 1868. In an attempt to settle the wars that had been raging since 1854. Land was sliced off the reservation granted to the Sioux and the food ration was cut down. The treachery of the whites, who had reneged on a treaty drawn up by themselves, was incomprehensible to the Sioux.

THE
ELEMENT
LIBRARY
NATIVE
AMERICAN
TRADITIONS

Bearheart, a Creek Indian, is a modern medicine man reviving traditional practices in the desert of New Mexico.

The recent resurgence in native traditions

Be this as it may, in the last half of the twentieth century many tribes have seen a renaissance of traditional ways. If on the one hand there has been a tendency toward pan-Indian movements like that focusing on the peyote rituals, on the other hand, many tribes have taken a renewed pride in the old ways. They have sought to restore their traditional religious and cultural practices, sometimes even by consulting the works of nineteenth-century white ethnographers and other like sources, if, for example, the elders are unable to remember rituals completely. There have

been renewed efforts to recover sacred lands taken from the native peoples, and to retain those lands threatened anew by white government or business.

Given such developments, one cannot but see as signs of hope the new interest shown by European-derived Americans in the traditional ways of native peoples. While one could hardly expect widespread 'conversions' to native ways, still it seems evident that the Native American views of nature and of spirituality are affecting white society in ways that previously would have been unthinkable. Some of this influence is rather superficial, of course, particularly that associated with so-called 'new age' true believers. But there is evidence that many Europeans and European-Americans are willing, indeed eager, to learn about traditional tribal spirituality.

In a book like this, it is impossible to do justice to the whole range of Native American traditions; one cannot begin to address all the different tribal practices and ways. There are, though, certain aspects of American Indian cultures that do transcend individual tribal differences, and that do allow one to speak in, more or less, general terms. We will also draw on the testimony of the most widely respected tribal spokesmen or visionaries: men like Black Elk and Thomas Yellowtail, whose significance transcends their particular tribal affiliations. While we cannot discuss the totality of American Indian traditions, we can discuss that which is perennial and universal within them.

Indeed, it is precisely what is universally applicable within the Native American traditions that we need to hear, in this time of social, economic, ecological, and above all, religious crises. What the Native Americans have to tell us speaks directly to our modern crises, and especially to our modern near-total divorce from the natural world. The American Indian religions are religions inextricably linked to nature, in mysterious ways that are only now beginning to be taken seriously by the dominant white society.

Hence this is a book of listening – listening to what virgin nature and the Native Americans have to tell us. Let us listen.

Traditional hunting and gathering skills

Warriors out alone shot wild
birds to feed themselves.

Hunting buffalo in winter. The
Indian hunters wore snowshoes and
worked as a team to kill the
buffalo trapped in drifting snow.

Women and children gathered fruit,
berries, nuts and wild grains such as
wild rice, a species of grass, despite
its name.

Indians from Virginia
fishing from canoes.

2

TRADITIONS
OF THE
NORTH AND SOUTH

Wary Eskimo children from the turn of the century, wrapped up against the big chill of Alaska in traditional animal skin clothes.

Although there is a certain artificiality in making divisions between northern and southern tribal traditions – particularly when some of the mid-western and south-eastern tribes include elements common to both northern and southern groups – the fact remains that such divisions do often hold true. Northern traditions, stretching from the sub-Arctic regions down through southern Canada and parts of the upper United States, are largely nomadic, shamanic and closely related to Siberian and Mongolian counterparts, while the southern traditions are marked by agriculture and large urban communities. In the chapter that follows we will discuss and explore each of these in greater detail, focusing on general tribal correlations and divergences.

THE NORTH

The Eskimo

Central among the far northern tribes are the Eskimo. Their existence in the deep cold, on the windswept coasts and along the icy seas of Alaska, is marked by a shamanism deeply akin to their Siberian counterparts. The Eskimo take their precarious livelihood from the often ice-covered oceans, and so it is not surprising that their cosmology – like their existence itself – is intimately related to the great waters. Indeed, chief in their cosmology is the Keeper or Master of the Animals, Takánakâpsaluk, Sedna, or Takanaluk, is a semi-aquatic, semi-human figure at the bottom of the ocean who controls the sea animals upon whom the Eskimo depend for their sustenance.

According to the Eskimo, the Sea Spirit or Keeper of the Sea Animals is affiliated with a young Eskimo woman who was thrown into the ocean by her father, and whose fingers were cruelly cut off when she clung to the side of the boat. In this image one can see something of why the ocean is considered both fickle and beneficent, the source of violent storms but also the source of food and other necessities of life. While the goodness of the sea's bounty comes from the sacrifice of the fingers, so too from the Sea Keeper comes misfortune and sickness and loss of the soul – the withholding of game.

Hence, like some of their Siberian shamanic counterparts, the Eskimo shaman often has to journey. His journey is down to the bottom of the ocean or under the ground, down to the centre where lives the Keeper of the Sea Animals or the Keeper of the Game Animals. This journeying is on an axis, or towards the axial centre of existence, the central concept which unites all the various American tribal groups, and indeed virtually all shamanism as well. A ceremony is held, the Eskimo shaman leaving the sacred area and going down under the earth and away from witnesses of the ceremony, the sound of his voice calling out 'ha-le-le'.[1]

Essentially, the shaman must go as the intermediary for someone who is sick, or for a family, or for an entire village, in order to make right the relationship between humans and the Keeper. Thus the shaman must overcome certain barriers on his way down, and when down, must perform certain ritual actions in order to redress breaches in the many taboos that the tribe must follow. During this time, the people present at the ceremony may have to confess their errors, vow not to repeat them, and sometimes even have to send out for someone who is absent, in order to receive a confession. In this way, people's transgressions are atoned for, and they are able to feel real relief at the ending of the Sea Keeper's anger.

From this example, we can see something of the precarious life that the Eskimo must live, existing as they do in a complex relationship with the countless souls of the animals upon whom they must nourish themselves. This is a central reason for many taboos, or prohibitions, that the Eskimo must observe, not for 'superstitious reasons', but precisely because they see the visible world as depending upon the invisible. To violate a

ABOVE *A shaman's rattle in the shape of a bird. Animal-shaped rattles were used to summon the spirit of the particular animal to allow the shaman to commune with it on behalf of the tribe.*

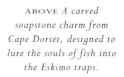

ABOVE *A carved soapstone charm from Cape Dorset, designed to lure the souls of fish into the Eskimo traps.*

THE
ELEMENT
LIBRARY
NATIVE
AMERICAN
TRADITIONS

taboo will have repercussions in the visible world, because the invisible world is always present and governs what humans experience. Likewise, to expiate a violation may in turn mean the end of a bad hunting situation.

This ever-present invisible reality explains the importance of the shaman, who acts as an interpreter of the unseen for the tribe, or for individuals in the tribe. Indeed, the shaman is often characterized as one who understands the 'secret language' of the animals; he is able to understand and converse with them in a

way that ultimately reflects the human condition in paradise, where all creatures understand one another and are at peace. This concept of a 'secret language' of nature is not limited to the Eskimo, it is found among many, and perhaps virtually all, indigenous peoples. However, among the Eskimo, the *angakut* or shaman makes contact with the souls he wishes to by using this secret language in a special song, so that the song is the medium by which the shaman begins to communicate with the invisible realm.

The Algonquin

As we move southwards and away from the far northern Arctic wastes, we enter the world of the Algonquin peoples. Like the Eskimo, they participate in the shamanic realm, but with some significant differences. For as we move southwards, we find an increasing ceremonialism, with more complex ritual traditions and a rich mythological tradition. Like the Eskimo, the Algonquin see in the natural world the manifestation of many spirits; and, in addition to shamanic means, have rituals that also perpetuate the balance between man and nature. One of these, that of the 'sweat

lodge', has as its purpose the purification of the individual, and the return to the primordial state of harmony between the elements of earth, air, fire and water.

The Algonquin peoples participate in the shamanic northern traditions, but with a central difference: rather than the shaman going on a journey of the soul, he calls the helping spirits into a central sphere. In this, the ceremony of the 'shaking lodge', or *jossakid*, we find the medium of connection between the human and invisible world; the helping spirits often make mysterious tapping or other sounds. Just as witnesses to Eskimo

Algonquin whalers return to shore in their impossibly small boat. The Algonquin used Shamanic rituals to help them in their whale hunt and to establish harmony between the hunter and the prey.

shamanic ceremonies have witnessed the shaman moving away to the other world, so too witnesses to Algonquin ceremonies have seen phenomena that cannot easily be explained. Often the shaman is bound with ropes for the ceremony but is released by the spirits while left alone in the darkness.

Here, as with the Eskimo, there are Keepers of the Game, or animal spirits, but with the Algonquin one also finds the presence of totems, which mark certain secret ceremonial lodges among the tribespeople. The totem represents a supraphysical affiliation that holds together a group of people who, while they may not be genetically related, regard one another as members of a given 'family' or lodge, and cannot marry within that lodge. Often, those who belong to a lodge profess a special affinity for their totem animal, a kind of supraphysical rapport with members of that species, and often there are dream or visionary connections. Totemic animals also proffer special kinds of knowledge particular to them and confer it on lodge members.

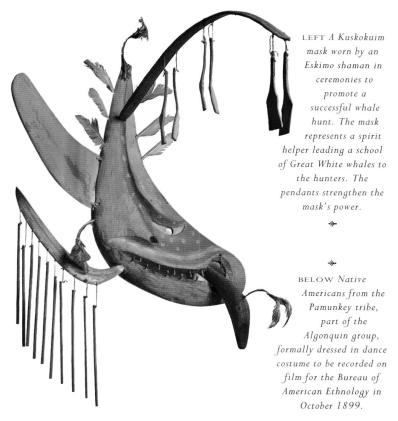

LEFT *A Kuskokuim mask worn by an Eskimo shaman in ceremonies to promote a successful whale hunt. The mask represents a spirit helper leading a school of Great White whales to the hunters. The pendants strengthen the mask's power.*

BELOW *Native Americans from the Pamunkey tribe, part of the Algonquin group, formally dressed in dance costume to be recorded on film for the Bureau of American Ethnology in October 1899.*

THE
ELEMENT
LIBRARY
NATIVE
AMERICAN
TRADITIONS

The Iroquois

If we travel yet further south – and east – into the eastern woodlands and the Great Lakes, we find there, even more socially and religiously complex societies. In the east we find the Iroquois nations with their confederacy, a governmental model that, it has been suggested, served as one source of inspiration for the form of government adopted by the United States. Like the Algonquin tribes, the Iroquois lived on a diet of maize, beans, squash, wild nuts, wild fruits and, of course, venison and small game.

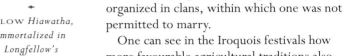

BELOW Hiawatha, immortalized in Longfellow's 'The Song of Hiawatha' (1855) was in reality a great Mohawk chief and founder of the Iroquois Confederacy.

BELOW RIGHT An Iroquois 'False Face', the iconic mask worn during religious ceremonies.

Matrilineal, they lived in lodges and were organized in clans, within which one was not permitted to marry.

One can see in the Iroquois festivals how more favourable agricultural traditions also produced a more complex religious calendar. The Iroquois celebrated the Strawberry Festival, the Bean Festival and the Maize Festival. They also had the 'False Face' Society, in which False Face dancers wore masks cut from living trees and manifested various supernatural beings. It is important to note – though we will come back to this at length later – that for tribal peoples generally, such masks do not merely 'represent' supernatural forces, but rather the icon, if we may so call it, manifests the force or being it depicts, and the dancer becomes it.

This brings us to the well-known Iroquois word *orenda*, which means spiritual power, and which is characteristic of certain ritual objects and also of people who have come to embody spiritual power. One can find equivalents to the word *orenda* in many other Native American languages; in Algonquin, for instance, the word is *manitou*. *Orenda* is the power of the 'other world' manifesting itself in this one, whether through ritual or other means. One may say that *orenda* represents a kind of psychic force, or field, and a manifestation of vital force.

The Ojibway, Chippewa, Ottawa and Potawatomi

Before they were sent to reservations in the landlocked Plains, the Indians who lived around the Great Lakes enjoyed freedom on the waters, using their canoes to move around and setting up temporary encampments while they hunted and fished.

West of the Iroquois – in the areas around the Great Lakes – are found the Ojibway, Chippewa, Ottawa and Potawatomi Indians. Some remain in their native area, though others were displaced to reservations as far away as Kansas. Among these groups were the Midê, or Midêwiwin, secret lodges, which were initiatory with hierarchic levels or degrees marked at the initial level by aquatic totems like the muskrat or beaver, at a higher level by birds, and at the highest level by the bear, the most sacred of animals. The Midê society, entry to which is progressively more expensive as one ascends degrees in the hierarchy, often draws those who are ill and who seek in it healing powers. Its highest members are considered to be shamans, or medicine men, and the Midê society as a whole may be seen as a ritualization of more individualistic shamanism.

Central to the Midê is the concept of regeneration or rebirth. The initiate is reborn through a ceremony in which he has sacred *me'gis* or cowrie shells 'shot' into him, so that he experiences spiritual death, falls down and is then raised up by the holy man. This ceremony has certain parallels with Australian Aboriginal traditions involving crystals that are also 'shot' into the initiate. The initiate is in this way made into a medicine man. Given that the Midê ceremonies take place in a great lodge, which represents in symbolic form the entire directional cosmos, given that entry requires purification, and finally, given the nature of the Mysteries performed inside, one may well say that the goal of the Midê society is the restoration of the paradisal state for its members – a restoration which has significant ramifications for both this life and for the next.

THE
ELEMENT
LIBRARY
NATIVE
AMERICAN
TRADITIONS

The Kwakiutl

Much further west, we find the Kwakiutl of Vancouver Island, who also have a secret or medicine society that offers initiation with ramifications both for this life and for the next. Among the Kwakiutl, this lodge is called the *hamatsa*, or cannibal society, and in it, initiation entails facing death and terror. The initiate goes into a lodge and, in an opening ceremony, hears the pipe of the *hamatsa* deity outside. Leaving the lodge, he is instructed in the ways of the fearsome deity who is affiliated with the celestial Pole or Axis, and who for the initiate also embodies death, and hence entails resurrection. The initiate returns to the lodge after having fasted and, in a trance state, having met the clan's guardian deity himself. Here the initiate embodies the

god who has seized him, and who slowly relinquishes his control of the initiate.

The Kwakiutl – and the Pacific Coast tribes more generally – are part of the Wakashan linguistic family, and although their secret societies show some parallels with those of their eastern brethren, some aspects of their culture are unique. These tribal peoples, live in large, split-plank dwellings, outside which one finds tall, ornately carved totem poles representing the clan to which that family or group belongs. Their livelihoods come in part, from fishing, either in the ocean or in rivers. Perhaps their most well known custom is the potlatch, in which a clan or clan leader will give away as many goods or gifts as he can; in this tradition, superiority comes not from what one can accumulate, but from what one can give away.

ABOVE LEFT
A Kwakiutl potlatch figure, a symbol of the custom of giving away as many worldly goods as possible.

TOP *Among the Haida of Queen Charlotte Island, the transformation of people into animals was an established tradition. In Haida legend, an adopted boy named Sîn was later revealed as a sky god and transformed himself into a woodpecker.*

ABOVE *The medicine man was a potent figure among the Indians of the north west coast. A powerful medicine man might visit other settlements, ferried in a ceremonially decorated canoe.*

The Plains tribes

East and south of the Pacific coast tribes are
those who together are called the Plains
tribes, including the Sioux, the Pawnee, the
Crow, the Kansa, the Dakota and the Mandan
tribes, to name only a few in this rich and
diverse group. Indeed, not only is it difficult
to name all the members of this broad and
most famous of the tribal groupings, but it is
also difficult to name all the sources for it.
The Plains Indians drew from both northern
and southern traditions. One finds in some of
their number, clear traces of ceremonies with
Aztecan or Mayan roots, while in others, one
finds more northern shamanic traditions.
Inasmuch as the Plains peoples were relatively
late in developing, depending as they did upon
the introduction of the horse, one is not
surprised that their historical affiliations, or
traditional roots, were somewhat far flung.

It is interesting that this Plains grouping is
most firmly fixed in the modern mind as
characteristic of Native Americans, not least

ABOVE *The gods of the
Dakota Sioux represented
every aspect of the
natural and
supernatural worlds.*

LEFT *Sioux Indians were
fierce warriors. They
were among the first to
learn to ride horses,
brought to America by
the Spanish and looked
upon by the Indians as a
'sacred dog'. Horse-
raiding, or rustling stock
from other tribes, was
common all over the
Great Plains.*

THE
ELEMENT
LIBRARY
NATIVE
AMERICAN
TRADITIONS

since historically it is a relatively late adaptation. However, one can explain this, not only because the Plains adaptations have been among the most spiritually vital of the tribal groups, but also because they were the tribal groups which most effectively opposed the movement of white settlers westwards, and which most effectively captured the imaginations of both Americans and Europeans. That the Plains tribes have been spiritually resilient is proven both by their historical flexibility, and by their serving as a source of spiritual renewal for many other American Indian groups.

There are several elements of Plains spirituality that remain pivotal for many tribes to this day. One is the ceremonial or sacred pipe, which represents the axial centre of the cosmos; pipe smoking seals agreements, and represents in symbolic form the breath of sacred creation. Black Elk told the story of how White Buffalo Calf Woman brought the sacred pipe to the Lakota people. Two hunters saw her approaching and one had bad thoughts for her. A cloud came down and when it lifted, he was nothing but bones being eaten by snakes. The holy woman came to the tribe

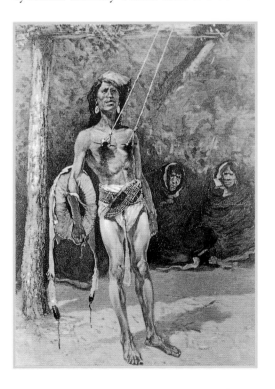

and gave them a sacred pipe, saying: 'Behold this pipe! Always remember how sacred it is, and treat it as such, for it will take you to the end. Remember in me there are four ages. I am leaving now, but I shall look back upon your people in every age, and at the end I will return.'[2] Thus to celebrate the sacred pipe is to return to this mythological irruption of the spiritual into the temporal world that White Buffalo Calf Woman represents.

Another element of Plains religion is the Sun Dance, which again reveals the axial centre of the cosmos, and which reminds us of the warrior ethos that guided the Plains peoples. The Sun Dance sometimes entails warriors piercing their chest muscles with thongs attached to the central pole, an act which in effect reaffirms the human connection to the centre and the primal sacrifice that is creation itself. Finally, one finds among the Plains tribes purification rites like that of the *inipi*, or 'sweat lodge', in

ABOVE *An old chief smokes a solitary sacred pipe in peace.*

LEFT *A Blackfoot warrior undergoes the ordeal of the Sun Dance. Tethered to a central pole by leather thongs skewered to his chest, he had to circle the pole from dawn to dusk, his eyes constantly fixed on the Sun.*

OPPOSITE *An Indian Council, painted by Seth Eastman in 1849.*

which the elemental or creational aspects of
the cosmos are recapitulated: stone, fire,
wood, air, water and earth.

In short, the Plains Indians incorporate
sacramental and shamanic elements from both
northern and southern traditions. While their
nomadic existence on the Plains resembles
northern tribes' nomadism, their agriculture
and some of their ceremonies – particularly
those of the Pawnee – derive from the
southern ritual cycles. In this respect, then,
the Plains tribes represent a natural transition
point for us, inasmuch as they combine
aspects of many different traditions, their very
existence being on land intermediate between
the mountains and the forests to the east,
midway between north and south. From them
we turn to the southern tribes proper.

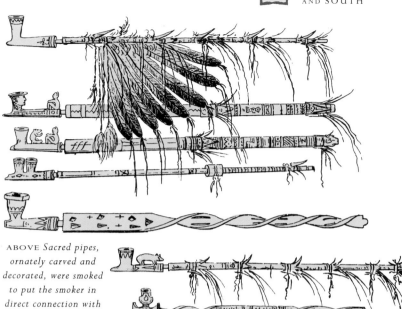

ABOVE *Sacred pipes,
ornately carved and
decorated, were smoked
to put the smoker in
direct connection with
the Great Spirit.*

THE
ELEMENT
LIBRARY
NATIVE
AMERICAN
TRADITIONS

THE SOUTH

ABOVE *Pueblo Indians lived in settled farming villages and their stable lives gave them time to develop skills such as pottery. Much of the decoration on their pots appears to be influenced by Mayan craftsmanship.*

Above all, the southern tribal groups in general differ from their northern counterparts by their communal social structure. Whereas the northernmost tribes tend to be much more inclined toward Arctic shamanic practices that have analogues in Siberia and northern Asia, and to be more nomadic hunters, the southern tribal groups, for all their differences, tended to be organized in large urban communities with an integrated priesthood and social-religious hierarchy. Certainly this is true of the 'high cultures' of Peru, Central America, and Mexico, the Mayas and the Incas, as well as of tribal groups of the southern United States, including the Pueblos.

Of course, the distinction we are making here is only true historically and not so true now. The Spanish conquest of some four hundred years ago meant the almost total destruction of many of these societies, at least as integrated urban cultures. Some have argued that the southern indigenous 'high cultures' of the Americas had become decadent, and hence were ripe for the destruction wrought by the Spanish subjugation. But whatever the reasons for this obliteration, we are left with much less

information about these cultures than we possess about the northern cultures, who were able to survive, albeit precariously, into the twentieth century.

For information about these urban southern cultures we must largely rely on only a few manuscripts, on the often dubious reports of missionaries and priests, and, needless to say, on the friezes, temples, pyramids and other artifacts that still remain. 'Popular native religions' do of course still remain throughout South and Central America, as well as in Mexico, but it is unclear how much of this 'residual religion' carries on the more ancient cultural and religious traditions. Certainly Roman Catholicism in Latin America has taken on indigenous functions, incorporating into altars, as well as dances and other cultural practices, elements that date back to before the Spanish conquest. But precisely what survived and how, and what changed in cultural practices, one cannot easily say.

But let us consider origins. Archaeologists have speculated a great deal about possible links between Far Eastern or Asian cultures

and early Mesoamerican traditions. Some archaeologists argue that, because of deep cultural similarities between various aspects of Chinese, Japanese, and Cambodian and Indian cultures – including metallurgy, ceramics, architecture and mythology – there was probably trans-Pacific travel and cultural insemination between 3000 and 2000 BC. It is very difficult to substantiate conclusively such controversial theories, but without question there are many parallels between Hindu, Buddhist and Mesoamerican cultures.

In any case, we will consider our southern tribal groups from the north southward, beginning with the Pueblo and in particular, the Hopi tribes of the southern United States, and then from their cultural origins as well.

The Pueblo

Like the more southern ancient tribal cultures of the Incas and Aztecs, the Pueblo are organized along stable agrarian and urban cultural lines. The Pueblo peoples – who remain a culturally diverse group – have retained their traditional ways, despite the anti-traditional attitudes of the United States government and various Christian missionary

BELOW *The Anasazi, ancestors of the Pueblo, lived in complex urban communities. They built houses directly into the cliffs for safety and shelter. The Cliff Palace is the largest remaining Anasazi dwelling at Mesa Verde National Park, Colorado.*

efforts. In part, the Pueblo were able to maintain their traditional practices and beliefs because although they appeared to acquiesce to outside demands, in fact they were able to continue their traditions in secret.

Pueblo traditions are based in a vertical 'emergence' cosmology. According to this, people emerged into the present material world from a less restricted, more sacred state of being. Indeed, Pueblo 'history' is really a recounting of these cosmological emergences, which bear a close resemblance to Greek, Hindu and Judaeo-Christian traditions regarding Gold, Silver, Bronze and Iron Ages. This is why Pueblo cosmology is not to be confused with modern evolutionist theories of 'progress', since traditionally our own present 'Iron Age' is not the culmination, but the worst of these Ages, one actually prophesied to come.

The Pueblo cosmology – like that of southern tribes generally – is represented by an axis along which these 'worlds' are arranged. A similar vertical cosmology is reflected in the pyramid temples of Central and South America. While the number of these worlds or spheres differs in some tribal groups – for the Zuni there are seven – their cosmological and axial significance remains fundamentally similar. This axial significance explains why the *kiva*, or underground chamber, is so significant for the Pueblo. To enter it is to place oneself precisely on this vertical axis and to enter the sacred womb of the earth, the sacred place of emergence.

But the richness of Pueblo cosmology cannot really be understood without reference to the mythological cycles and legends, within which the real meaning of man's place on earth, the heavens, the sun and the animals is contained. Through the complex annual cycles of masked dances and ceremonies, as well as through the myths that inform these cycles, each participant is shown his true place and purpose on this earth. These cycles and masked dances represent the union – the indivisibility – of the human, the animal, the spirit and the celestial worlds; they form a liturgical cycle that in fact reveals spiritual presences in the natural and human world.

THE
ELEMENT
LIBRARY
NATIVE
AMERICAN
TRADITIONS

The Olmec

When one moves from the southern United States into Mexico and Central America, one moves into a different, but certainly related, far older cultural context. The tribes of Mexico, including the developed urban culture of the Aztec, derived from an earlier 'mother culture', that of the Olmec. Of course, we cannot determine with precision exactly what cosmological and cultural traditions the Olmecs held, since they were a highly developed but non-writing culture. Yet like the Pueblo, and indeed like all the southern tribal groups, their culture was a complex interweaving of celestial, animal, natural and human aspects or symbols.

The Olmec flourished between 1800 and 300 BC and are most famous for their colossal art, including not only the well-known 'Olmec heads', but many other figures as well, some carved into the earth itself. Many readers may be familiar with the enormous 'Olmec heads', colossal basalt heads standing more than three metres high, found along the Mexican Gulf Coast. Not so familiar, however, are the stylized carvings into the earth itself, the countless *stelae* (carved upright stones), the sacred caves and chambers, and other cultural remains that bespeak a culture closely intertwined with the animal and spirit worlds.

Indeed, this interconnection between the human, the animal and the spirit worlds permeates the whole of Mesoamerican tribal cultures. The Olmec representations of jaguar-humans, bird-humans and serpent-humans certainly reveal a culture in which the spirit world – after all, the origin of the human and natural worlds – appeared to human beings in anthropomorphic and theriomorphic forms. The animal-human images probably represent spirit helpers of the shamans or priests as well. But in any case, in them we see the archetypal forms of beings who are 'above', and inform both the human and natural worlds.

The Olmec culture shows us how highly developed a culture can be without writing, evidenced not least by the late Olmec and Mayan astrological calculations. Like their

LEFT *An Olmec ceremonial axe carved in jade. Ritual weapons such as this may have been used in sacrificial rites.*

successors the Maya, the Olmec were apparently deeply concerned with sidereal and planetary cycles, and their religious cycles were bound up with those of the heavens. One might say that the Olmec and their successors were so concerned with celestial cycles because, by understanding these cycles, they could be aligned with greater forces, and the terrestrial world could be in harmony with the celestial. Some archaeologists argue that the Mayan astrological system derived from that of the Olmec.

The Maya

Although we do not know precisely what the cultural relationship between the Olmec and the Maya was – how the Maya inherited their traditions from the Olmec – still it is generally acknowledged that, in the Maya, Mesoamerican native traditions reached their cultural apogee. Among the Olmec appeared the great temples and works of art, the theocratic state organization, the priestly hierarchy, the system of hieroglyphics and numbers, the calendrical calculations and the theriomorphic humans or spirit-beings characteristic of all later 'high cultures' of Mesoamerica. Among the Maya these characteristics flowered.

Certainly the 'classic Maya', who flourished between AD 200 and 900, produced a remarkable civilization, no less extraordinary because it appeared in a jungle environment

BELOW *The plumed serpent, called Quetzalcoatl by the Aztecs, was a recurring figure in the South American pantheon. The god of learning and priesthood, he was also an aspect of the sun god.*

usually not conducive to intensive urban complexes like those of the Maya. The Mayan civilization, with its large urban complexes and lavish temples and ceremonies, its class system and its intricate astrological calendar, reveals a stable traditional society of great complexity. The magnitude of this culture is exemplified by the great city of Teotihuacan, a sacred city organized as a quadripartite image of the cosmos as a whole, an astonishing architectural marvel centred around the *axis mundi*, or axial centre of the cosmos, the 'cosmic tree' recognized in many cultures around the world.

Probably the greatest achievement of this culture – which in many ways resembles that of classical Hindu India – was its knowledge of astrological cycles. The Maya developed their sidereal calculations to a high art and, like the Hindus, were able to recognize our present astrological cycle within much larger cycles. They were able to recognize daily astrological patterns or currents of force, as well as annual and longer patterns. According to the Mayan calculations, called the 'long count', our current time cycle began in 3114 BC, and will end on 23 December 2012. But the Mayan priests again like the Hindus, also calculated on a much larger scale, calculations of cycles going back to nine million years BC having been found in ceremonial centres.

ABOVE *The Temple of Warriors at Chichen Itza, believed to have been built by the Toltecs. It is guarded by a Chac Mool figure, thought to be a receptacle for the human hearts torn out in sacrifice to the gods.*

LEFT *The Mayan maize god. Maize was a staple food for the Maya and the spirit of the maize god was invoked to ensure good harvests.*

No one knows precisely why the Mayan culture collapsed around AD 900. Some speculate that this collapse was due to agricultural factors, others that political, economic and religious crises converged to bring about social disaster. Not all aspects of the classic Mayan culture disappeared with this collapse: for instance, one finds the classic Mayan calendar survived in the Yucatan into the modern era; and certainly many cultural elements were not only inherited by later traditions, but were carried on in diaspora. However, as an integrated, highly complex religious and cultural organization, the classic Mayan civilization did not last beyond the tenth century AD.

THE
ELEMENT
LIBRARY
NATIVE
AMERICAN
TRADITIONS

The Aztec and the Inca

The classic Mayan culture was succeeded by that of the Aztecs, which looked back to the great city of Teotihuacan and to the intervening Toltec cultural group as its origin. Aztec culture, which flourished between AD 1325 and 1521, based its cultural history on the cultural group that formed around the sacred kingdom of Tollan after the collapse of Teotihuacan. According to Aztec tradition, the Toltecs were ruled for a time by a sacred man-god, Quetzalcoatl, 'The Prince of the Plumed Serpent', who had a miraculous birth, went through a period of asceticism, was a fierce warrior and finally king of the empire. Aztecs held that from him descended 'all the arts and sciences'. They also believed that he would return again; and hence the Aztecs at first greeted Cortes and his men as the returning Quetzalcoatl and his retinue, although they found out quickly enough that Cortes signalled not the renewal, but the collapse of their culture.

From what we have said already, it is clear that Mesoamerican traditions went through many periods of cultural renewal, and certainly the Aztec, like the Toltec and Mayan before them, represented such a period. However, even taking into account the many cultural confluences from which the Aztecs drew, one can say with certainty that they represented an extremely warlike and cruel religious tradition, even compared with cultures from which it inherited astrological, religious and artistic traditions.

The Aztecs were a very developed urban society, with an extremely complex theocratic hierarchy and religious tradition; but they were also given to making sacrifices, including human sacrifice. In this practice, the Aztecs have many analogues around the world; but Aztecan sacrifice was perhaps the most widespread and deeply rooted in cultural significance. Essentially, human sacrifice was based on the idea of cosmic equilibrium; the practice was intended to rectify imbalances in cosmic forces, to reinforce cosmic forces that otherwise might career out of order. The Aztec cosmos was one of precariously balanced order and harmony; a sacrifice meant the releasing of certain energy that, dedicated to a particular god or force, helped maintain its power.

These sacrifices took a remarkable range of forms, from the most well known – the cutting out of the victim's heart – to hurling from heights, strangulation, burning,

decapitation and arrow sacrifice. There was also the regular practice of autosacrifice, or ritual bloodletting, practised by warriors, priests or nobility. Sometimes, for example, men bled their penises, in a kind of ritual practice that engendered cosmic rejuvenation. This idea of cosmic rejuvenation is central not only to these forms of sacrifice, but to the whole Aztecan cosmology, which was based on the idea that sacrifice, order and the reinforcing of the cosmic vitality or order, were all deeply intertwined.

The Aztecan culture was a warrior culture par excellence, a warrior culture based precisely on these concepts of sacrifice, order and cosmic revitalization. Although we will discuss Native American warrior customs in our next chapter, we will consider Aztec warriorship here because it is so deeply a part of this cultural tradition. The Aztecs regarded war in the light of cosmic sacrifice; to kill one's enemies, or to be killed, was part of the greater cosmic harmony, and the 'paying of one's debt to the cosmos'. What to modern people may appear as slaughter takes on a ritual and spiritual significance, and in fact this is why warriors (in Aztec as in European traditions) would always prefer a noble death to an ignoble life.

ABOVE RIGHT *Aztec society was extremely hierarchical and dominated by the warrior class. To be a warrior or priest (or both) was considered the only fit activity for a man.*

RIGHT *Human sacrifice was considered essential to the harmony of the cosmos. The Aztecs believed that they had a special duty to the gods, to feed them blood. If they failed, the Sun would not rise, and the universe would end.*

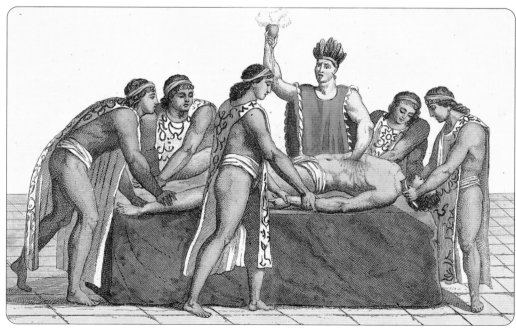

The Aztecs warred also to augment and preserve political boundaries, but warfare was primarily seen in a ritual and, indeed, poetic light. While warring against one's enemies did establish order in a given area when the war was concluded, and of course allowed victors to gain spoils or tribute as well as sacrificial victims, the battleground was also the place where the 'jaguars roared', and one series of battles was even described as 'the flowery wars' (1450-1519). Warriors were directed by *tlatoanis*, or king-speakers, and fought under the aegis of clans like the eagle and the jaguar. This reminds us again of how the entire tradition must be seen in the light of what is called 'cosmovision', meaning the totality of cosmological ritual and spiritual understanding that informed all the art, war, politics and other aspects of the culture.

This cosmovision concept suggests that although war was a central element of Aztec culture, it ought not be seen as the only element. For Aztec culture also produced magnificent temples and temple art, beautiful poetry and a spiritual tradition that allowed its practitioners to realize certain spiritual stations while still alive. If the warrior tradition was bloody, it was counterbalanced by an essentially stable, and certainly complete, cosmological and spiritual vision incorporated into the entire culture, a culture whose achievements were remarkable.

But like the Inca culture to the south, in Peru – which also flourished at the time of the Spanish conquest in the sixteenth century AD, and which was also a theocratic state organized around a single ruler identified with the sun – the Aztec culture fell quickly under the Spanish assault. The Aztecs, like the Incas, had little defence against the capture of their ruler or ruling class; if the strength of these cultures was their centralization in every sphere, from politics to art to religion, this was also their weakness, for under the Spanish, Catholicism was quickly instituted, and the temples to the gods of the Aztec and Inca replaced by churches or monasteries.

Of both the Inca and the Aztec, primarily the popular forms of religion remain, incorporated into Catholicism in ways that are to some extent paralleled by the way Christianity in Ireland became Celtic Christianity. Of course, many elements of the 'high cultures' of the Inca and Aztec are gone because the civilizations that supported them fell. But sacred sites remain sacred under the new religion and, indeed, the most famous spiritual manifestation in Latin America, that of the Virgin of Guadalupe, appeared just ten years after the arrival of Cortes at a hill dedicated to the Aztec goddess Tonantzin, suggesting again the deep continuity between indigenous Latin American religions and the Catholicism brought from Spain.

With these remarks, then, we end our geographical overview of the indigenous Indian traditions in the Americas. While there is certainly diversity among these many cultural groups, we can make general distinctions between northern and southern traditions, referring to the axial, communitarian southern groups, and to the more individualistic, shamanic northern groups. What is more, despite the enormous diversity of the many tribes, we can also examine some essential aspects of their common worldview. For although there are countless divergences between various tribes, all the tribes share certain characteristics when contrasted with the modern world. And it is to one such central characteristic that we now turn: warriorship.

3

THE WARRIOR

Most modern people are unfamiliar with the principles informing a warrior culture. Although our technological society has developed extraordinarily sophisticated ways of killing many people at once, this capacity is accompanied by anonymity. There is neither heroism nor valour in the dropping of a bomb, and this is precisely why the modern era is the age of mass murders on a scale previously incomprehensible.[3] We like to believe that warrior cultures are 'primitive' or even 'barbaric' and excessively cruel, without recognizing that our own 'progress' has brought about a world in which genocide is thinkable in ways previously impossible. To understand the warrior culture that informed many Native American traditions, we need to jettison the preconceptions of our modern world and consider what warriorship in a traditional culture really means.

WITH RED SPOT
'KILLED AN ENEMY'

'KILLED AN ENEMY AND
TOOK HIS SCALP'

'CUT AN ENEMY'S
THROAT'

'THIRD COUP'

'FOURTH COUP'

'FIFTH COUP'

'HAS BEEN WOUNDED
MANY TIMES'

TWO RED STRIPES
'THIRD COUP'

ABOVE *Indian warriors signalled their military history and prowess by wearing feathers of different kinds, cut and painted in various ways.*

◆

LEFT *Keokuk, chief of the Sauk and Foxes, in full warrior gear.*

◆

THE
ELEMENT
LIBRARY
NATIVE
AMERICAN
TRADITIONS

Great Indian Warriors

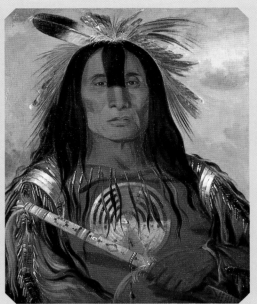

*Big Elk of the Omaha.
His dramatic black painted face shows he
has just killed an enemy in battle.*

*Buffalo Bill's Back Fat of the Blood or
Blackfoot division, in formal dress.*

*Florida Indian of the
16th century, armed with a
longbow.*

*Sioux and Snake Indians on the warpath. Sioux warriors were fast, skilful riders and
used their horses as shields in the heat of battle.*

THE AFTERLIFE AND SACRED PROTECTION

Warrior cultures are found world wide — including ancient northern European tribal traditions — and are based on certain common principles, chief among which is that of the afterlife. Certainly the Lakota Sioux, the Pawnee, the Huron, or the Aztec warriors would all have immediately understood the aphorism found in Beowulf, the Old English poem, that a noble death is far better than a shameful life. This basic idea informs all traditional warrior cultures, including Native American: that one's conduct in this life — of which war is the crucible and finest test — has ramifications beyond this life. Hence one can say that the afterlife is determined by our conduct here on earth.

From this basic principle derives the extraordinary heroism that typifies so many Native American traditions. One has countless examples of Native American warriors accomplishing remarkable feats of heroism, facing battle with bravery and equanimity — precisely because these warriors rested assured that this present life is a kind of proving ground, fleeting and possessed of significance because it unfolds into the afterlife. This emphasis on nobility and bravery in single combat brought about, for example, the Plains Indian tradition of

'counting coup', meaning that one would tap or strike one's enemy in battle with a 'coup stick'. This practice underscores the fact that what matters in battle is not necessarily killing but proving one's mettle in combat, a belief that has analogues in a number of tribes.

But the supernatural world, or the afterlife, is not separate from this world. One sees this in the practice of the 'Ghost Dance', which spread across tribes in the central United States during the late nineteenth century. Central to the Ghost Dance was the prophet Wovoka, who preached the coming apocalypse and a renewed world. The dance spread so quickly across tribal America precisely because it drew on the fundamental ideas of the indigenous warrior culture, one of which was that the spiritual world takes precedence over and informs the physical world. This in turn led to the belief, especially among the Sioux, that 'ghost shirts'; would render warriors invulnerable in battle.

Black Elk, the famous Sioux, spoke of how, just before the ill-fated battle at Wounded Knee between the cavalry and the Sioux he put on his sacred shirt which protected him. His sacred shirt was decorated with the images of his sacred vision, and so when Black Elk went into battle, although the bullets

ABOVE *An Arapaho ghost shirt, decorated with its owner's Sacred Vision. Ghost shirts were worn in the Ghost Dance and in battle, where they were believed to protect the wearer from harm.*

RIGHT *The Scalp Dance celebrates victory after a fierce skirmish.*

THE
ELEMENT
LIBRARY
NATIVE
AMERICAN
TRADITIONS

whizzed around him, he was not hurt. 'All the time the bullets were buzzing around me and I was not hurt. I was not even afraid. It was like being in a dream about shooting.'[4] But suddenly, it was as though his dream evaporated, he was afraid, and in that moment of vacillation he was wounded by a bullet. This battle, he said, at which Sioux women and children were also killed, marked the end of the old Sioux culture.

Such remarkable instances of sacred protection in warfare are not restricted to the Ghost Dance, to Black Elk, or to the 'old days'. Thomas Yellowtail, a contemporary Crow medicine man, tells us that during the Vietnam war, a young Crow went to Vietnam wearing a medicine feather, 'just like the medicine that warriors carried into battle in the old days'.[5] The young man was indeed protected, even though many of his company were mown down by machine-gun fire. Once

he was even shot at close range, but 'that bullet had ricocheted and didn't hurt him; it didn't penetrate his body even though it left a bullet hole through his shirt'.[6]

Remarkable events like this of course violate a materialist concept of the cosmos. We don't want to acknowledge that such miraculous events might in fact take place, for this in turn would suggest that the spiritual beliefs of religious people are indeed valid, and not merely 'superstition' no longer acceptable in our technological world. Miraculous events like those related by Black Elk and Thomas Yellowtail are attested to by all the Native American traditions, all of which have their shamans or medicine men or priests, and all of which acknowledge the priority of the realms of soul and spirit over the physical. It is on this priority that the traditional American Indian view of warfare is solidly based.

BELOW *The Dog Dance of the Dakota (Sioux) involved eating parts of the dog and re-enacting the feats of bravery. The Sioux feel that this way they can take on the bravery of the dog.*

BELOW RIGHT *In the Mandan rainmaking ritual, braves took it in turns to stand on a lodge roof invoking the rain god. Great honour went to the brave whose prayers produced the rain.*

STOICISM AND SELF-DISCIPLINE

Even if the tribal view of warfare is founded on the ideas of the afterlife, and on the governance of the physical world by spiritual and subtle forces, it cannot be denied that there is a cruel side to many indigenous cultures. We have already noted the apparent cruelty of the Aztec culture, based as it was on the idea of sacrifice, both of self and of others. But there are countless other examples of warrior stoicism in the face of terrible tortures among many tribes – and of the corresponding infliction of terrible tortures by both women and men. Many tribes would flay or mutilate captive enemies, practices that from a warrior perspective allow one to demonstrate one's stoicism in the face of the most terrible physical abuse. This stoicism derives from the code of noble conduct, from the recognition of the afterlife, and from magical protection.

    This code of noble conduct also reflects an insistence on self-discipline. The very first European explorers to arrive on Latin American soil observed the tribal practices of fasting, purification and vision seeking. These practices of self-purification or self-discipline are found among all Native American traditions, from those of the eastern woodlands to the prairies and the north country, down to the far southern tribes or

ABOVE *During peaceful times, warriors honed their coordination skills with games such as hoop-and-pole and racket ball, shown here, an early form of lacrosse.*

cultures. The harshest outward sacrifices, like those found in warfare, derive from and reflect this inward warfare, based in the conquering of individual desires or selfishness.

    To us – who hail from a technological society bent on providing creature comforts of every description, including even protection from extremes in temperature – the warrior code of conduct and the extreme behaviour it generates may seem unfamiliar. In a warrior culture, warfare and even torture provide tests of mettle; these are the extremes of human life that, while cruel, allow human beings a kind of latitude to test themselves against the very harshest of circumstances. While a world with air conditioning provides comfort and insulation from suffering, from a warrior perspective this comfort not only isolates us from the natural world, but even reduces the range of opportunities we have to prove our mettle. The warrior would say that a world without opportunities for heroism is a world of reduced opportunities to be human.

    Not all of the American Indian tribes have extreme warrior traditions. Those of the far north, for example, like the Eskimo, have a code of noble conduct, but nature's icy

THE
ELEMENT
LIBRARY
NATIVE
AMERICAN
TRADITIONS

In 1872 gold was discovered in Paha Sapa, the sacred Black Hills of Dakota and the Sioux were herded off their own land on to reservations to make way for white immigrant gold diggers. Sitting Bull and Crazy Horse urged their people to fight back. Colonel George Custer led troops against the Indians. On June 25 1876, at the Little Bighorn river, he encountered a Sioux war band. Not one white man of the Colonel's 250 soldiers survived.

harshness itself provides their test of mettle more than war. And, some tribes were more agrarian and peaceful, while others were more bent on marauding. However, there is always a code of conduct governed by a recognition of the afterlife which results in stoicism and acts of valour, whether tested against the natural world or against other people in warfare.

In Native American traditions, there is a fundamental unity recognized between the human world, the natural world, and the realms of spirits, that is in turn reflected in attitudes towards warfare. Among the Zuni, for instance, the Bow or War Priests have the specific function of directing the souls of slain enemy warriors (Apache or Navajo) back to Zuni, and converting these souls into bringers of rain through special retreat and purification ceremonies.[7] Essentially, such practices suggest the conversion of potentially violent and destructive powers into beneficent natural forces, particularly those of lightning and rain.

This interconnection between natural, human and spiritual cycles reflects the interwoven relationships among these realms, and reminds us again of how inseparable these three cycles really are in Native American traditions. If nature itself sometimes has a harsh or apparently cruel quality – seen in the animals of prey, for instance – it is not surprising that the same uncompromising quality occasionally appears in tribal cultures, or again in religious traditions themselves.

It is no doubt hard for us – conditioned as we are to think in exclusionary categories of nature as 'mechanism', of religion as 'separate' from nature and of human behaviour as increasingly separate from nature and from religious culture – to affirm the world view that produces the warrior code common to so many Native American traditions. But it is essential to at least recognize origins and significance of this code, for it may well have ramifications for us today, regardless of our historical situation.

4

HIEROPHANIC NATURE

The word 'hierophany' means, roughly, 'spiritual revelation'. While there are countless differences among the many tribal traditions of the Americas, nonetheless all the Native American traditions share a common recognition of nature as being informed by spiritual significance. What is more, there are certain animals, landforms and other manifestations of nature that embody spiritual significance for tribal peoples across almost the entire length and breadth of the Americas. Eagles, and many other creatures, not only bear spiritual significances, but can in fact be the manifestations of spirits themselves. In order to understand something of Native American traditions, then, one must come to recognize what is meant by the term hierophanic nature.

The Golden Eagle, perceived as a manifestation of a strong spiritual presence as well as a powerful bird of prey active in the real world.

THE
ELEMENT
LIBRARY
NATIVE
AMERICAN
TRADITIONS

NATURE AS A SPIRITUAL BEING

ABOVE *Opaina Indians dance to propitiate nature, manifested as a multitude of spirits.*

There are certain creatures and landforms that always possess a special significance for tribal peoples: the eagle, the hawk, the crow, the owl, the muskrat, the otter, the deer, the buffalo, mountains, rivers, bluffs and rocks. All have spiritual significance that is linked to particular tribal traditions and local geography or characteristics. Although the names and special significances of these creatures may differ, underlying the many diverse traditions there is a recognition of how the natural world bodies forth the invisible realms. A hawk is a hawk, but it also possesses profound spiritual significance, and sometimes, for example, is a manifested spirit-being come as a protector. In short, nature is also spiritual revelation.

It should also be emphasized that nature and certain of nature's creatures in a mysterious way truly manifest – that is, truly are – spiritual beings. This is perhaps not easy for us to acknowledge. Thomas Yellowtail, a Crow medicine man, tells how he went to gather special sacred medicine plants from a particular place. When he arrived there, he saw two eagles, one a golden eagle and one a bald eagle, watching over him. He recognized that these two eagles were 'working together', to protect the sacred plants, and he offered up a prayer to thank them for their spiritual presence. Those eagles were real, but

The Eagle and the Sun

THE EAGLE, AS THE HIGHEST FLYING AND NOBLEST BIRD OF PREY, IS ALWAYS ASSOCIATED WITH THE SUN AND WITH THE HIGHEST SPIRITUALLY DISCERNING POWER IN MAN. JOSEPH EPES BROWN DISCUSSES THIS SYMBOLISM IN *THE SACRED PIPE*, THE BOOK OF BLACK ELK'S WORDS ON SIOUX SACRED RITES:

Since Wanbli Galeshka (the Spotted Eagle) flies the highest of all created creatures and sees everything, he is regarded as Wakan-Tanka under certain aspects. He is a solar bird, his feathers being regarded as rays of the sun, and when it is carried or worn by the Indian it represents, or rather, is the 'Real Presence'. In wearing the eagle-feathered 'war bonnet', the wearer actually becomes the eagle, which is to say that he identifies himself, his real Self, with Wakan-Tanka. The Spotted Eagle corresponds exactly, in the Hindu tradition, to the Buddhi, which is the Intellect, or formless and transcendent principle of all manifestation; further, the Buddhi is often expressed as directly emanating from the Atma, the spiritual sun. From this it should be clear what is really being expressed in the often misunderstood Ghost Dance song: 'Wanbli galeshka wana ni he o who e', 'The Spotted Eagle is coming to carry me away.'[8]

THIS EXPLANATION SUGGESTS HOW MANY LEVELS OF SYMBOLISM EXIST IN THE TRIBAL VIEW OF CREATURES LIKE THE EAGLE, AND HOW PROFOUND THIS SYMBOLISM REALLY IS.

they were also spiritual presences. Yellowtail tells us how an interloper came to this place without being spiritually prepared, and how the eagles actually attacked him, driving him off. Every time Yellowtail goes to this place to gather sacred medicine plants, the eagles are there, watching from above.[9]

One must understand that nature is, in Native American traditions, the theatre in which the spirit realms and the human world intersect. The physical world is a material reflection of its archetypes. In tribal traditions, as in Islam, Christianity and the other world religions, we are taught that this world in which we live is not the only world. In fact, there are three worlds or realms: the physical, the subtle and the spiritual, in Hinduism called earth, atmosphere and sky. Of these, the physical realm is the smallest, and also the densest. But it is also the reflection and manifestation of higher realms.[10] So in a sense, nature is like the theatre in which the higher realms can be seen acting, having their effects. This is the profound meaning of sacred mask dances held by so many tribes, in which we see the higher powers taking on physical form before us in masked dancers.[11]

In Native American traditions, as in other world religions, we find a visionary spirituality that affirms the existence of an 'other world', an archetypal world that is 'more real' and 'more alive' than this physical world. Black Elk, for example, spoke of his life's greatest vision, and said that exactly at its culmination: 'I saw more than I can tell, and I understood more than I saw; for I was seeing in a sacred manner the shapes of all things in the spirit'.[12] What he saw was, he tells us, more beautiful than the things of earth can be; he saw the archetypal realm, the 'shapes of all things in the spirit'.

Yellowtail affirms the same reverence for nature we see in Black Elk and many other medicine men and tribal leaders. This reverence for nature derives from the realization that nature is hierophanic, that it reflects and bodies forth the realm of the spirit. As Yellowtail tells us:

⊚⊘

A man's attitude toward the Nature around him and the animals in Nature is of special importance, because as we respect our created world, so also do we show respect for the real world that we cannot see.[13]

⊚⊘

Certainly, then, the American Indian reverence for nature is not a matter of 'heathen idolatry', as some Christians once held, nor of 'worshipping divinized nature', as anthropologists once tried to assert. Rather, for tribal peoples nature is metaphysically transparent, and in it they recognize the manifestations of spiritual reality.

BELOW *Native American culture has little of its tradition recorded in writing by the Indians themselves. Theirs was an oral tradition, with tales of bravery in battle and sacred visions being told and retold until everyone knew them. Here, Mandan warriors gather after battle to 'record' their deeds in story form.*

THE
ELEMENT
LIBRARY
NATIVE
AMERICAN
TRADITIONS

NATIVE AMERICAN SACRED SITES

The legendary Cave of the Winds in the sacred Black Hills was central to Sioux beliefs. The entrance to it was a small hole. According to Sioux tradition, it was the gateway to the happy hunting ground.

There are some places in the virgin wilderness that are especially sacred, because they are the confluence of natural landforms and spiritual currents or forces. For example, one finds sandstone outcroppings with certain directional orientations – due south, sometimes – on which appear petroglyphs, hieroglyphic marks revealing the presence of certain spirits in that place. For the most part, such sites have been destroyed by unthinking modern tourists, who deface the petroglyphs with graffiti and even gunshots. One finds high bluffs used for the practice of 'lamenting for a vision', a practice common to many tribes.[14] Again, however, highways or other modern additions often render these sites unusable as well.

Indeed, a Supreme Court decision in 1988 focused on exactly such a controversy over a holy site in northern California, sacred to the Yurok, Karok and Tolowa Indians. In this landmark decision (which is reprinted as an appendix to my *Sacred Earth: The Spiritual Landscape of Native America*) the United States Supreme Court decided that despite the constitutional right to freedom of religious practice in America, and despite the absence of any compelling social or economic necessity, the United States Forest Service nonetheless had the right to cut timber in an area used by generations of tribal people for vision seeking. What is worse, the Forest Service was given permission to put a road through this sacred area, even though there was no need for such a road.[15]

Dissenting Justice William Brennan, joined by Thurgood Marshall and Harry A. Blackmun, offered a compelling and eloquent argument against the effective destruction of the Indian sacred site and, by extension, of the Indians' freedom to practise their religion.

Respondents here have demonstrated that completion of the ... road will completely frustrate the practice of their religion ... will virtually destroy respondents' religion, and will necessarily force them into abandoning those practices altogether ...

How, Brennan asks, can the government claim it is not affecting the tribal freedom to practise religion? The Court's decision is thus 'wholly untenable ... demonstrated by the cruelly surreal result it produces here: governmental action that will virtually destroy a religion is nevertheless deemed not to "burden" that religion'.

The sacred site in northern California being defiled as a result of this decision is, Brennan notes, critical to the practice of native religion there, particularly the celebration of World Renewal ceremonies. According to these tribes, the most sacred of lands is the high country where, they believe, prehuman spirits moved with the coming of humans to the earth. These spirits are the source of 'medicine', or spiritual power, and although only a few tribal members travel to the high country for medicine and spiritual renewal, the entire tribe's welfare hinges on the success of individual practitioners. This success, in turn, requires privacy, silence and an undisturbed natural setting. By destroying this site, the government is indeed effectively destroying the Native American religion from which this site is indivisible.

Among other things, then, we can see in this example not only the inherent conflict between modernity and traditional tribal practices, but what is more, the meaning of hierophanic nature for these tribal peoples. For these people travel to a given sacred site because that site provides contact with the spiritual world – much as a Christian might go to a cathedral. Nature itself – untouched, virgin nature – provides the tribal cathedral; it offers contact with the 'medicine fathers', or beneficent spirits. It is true that certain spirits may be called into even a relatively modern setting in some traditions – but it is in virgin nature that people can commune most closely with spiritual truth in its primordial simplicity and mystery.

There are so few sacred sites left now in the United States, that one would hope the government – ostensibly the guardian of the public trust – would help to preserve rather than to destroy them. But the American record in recognizing hierophanic natural places is not good. Virtually every single sacred site one might visit has been defiled in some way, and many have been destroyed outright. The most sacred spring in the Plains states – Wakonda Spring, a site sacred to many Plains tribes – was first made into a health spa, surrounded by a cement retainer, then filled with local concrete and trash, and finally buried underwater by Glen Elder Reservoir, a dam project completed in the mid-twentieth century.

It is true that there is a wide range of American Indian spiritual practices, and that there is great diversity in the specific ways tribes view animals and the natural world. But underlying these diversities of practice and of specific terms, there is a fundamental unity, certainly by comparison to the modern view of nature. For without question, all the traditional tribal peoples share a reverence for the natural world, and an awareness of its hierophanic possibilities. They recognize sacred places, places where man can come more easily in contact with spiritual forces, and they have the sense not to disturb or destroy these places. Perhaps we may yet learn from them this lesson.

The Kivas of the Anasazi were round subterranean chambers built for a ritual or religious purpose, but their precise function is unknown. On the floor of the Kiva was a small shallow hole, the sipapu, symbolizing the site of the people's emergence.

5

SPIRITS
AND
ANCESTORS

A Huron hunter blows sacred smoke into the mouth of a bear he has just killed to make peace with the animal's departed spirit.

Native American traditions are certainly not the only traditions to recognize our world as the theatre of spirit-beings, nor to reverence the path, the knowledge and rituals, handed down from their ancestors. Chinese, Hindu, Buddhist, Australian Aboriginal, Celtic, northern European, Greek – the list of peoples who hold such beliefs is certainly not small. But while there is great diversity among these many traditional cultures, and indeed, as we have seen, among the many different American Indian cultures as well, there are certain premises basic to all these traditions, especially regarding spirits and ancestors.

For Native American peoples, there is no clear division between human beings and the spirit world. That is, in general, it is possible for spirits to contact human beings and to affect human life. In many traditions, spirits not only contact human beings, but even take possession of them for certain sacred times. This is, as we said elsewhere, the esoteric meaning of mask dances, which are not merely dances for 'entertainment', but the actual manifestation on earth of the beings represented by the masks. In short, the human world in these traditions is 'permeable', in that spirit-beings can come into it and leave again.

THE KACHINAS

It is possible – at least in many traditions – for the dead to become spirit-beings. This is not to say that all dead become such spirit-beings – in a number of traditions, for instance the Hopi, it is held that some people die and are reincarnated again in another form in another world, while other people become spirit-beings in Hopi tradition, *kachinas*. There are many *kachinas*, a word that derives from *ka* (respect) and *china* (spirit). Some have counted 220, some more than 300 *kachinas*. But however many there are, *kachinas* are not only spirits of the dead, but spirits of animals, plants, minerals, stars and natural forces.

The *kachinas* underscore for us once again how the spirit world, the natural world and the human world intertwine for Native American peoples. To speak of an animal may also be to speak of a spirit manifesting itself in that animal; to speak of a spirit may also be to speak of one's ancestors, or of the mythological human 'prehistory' or, as Henry Corbin called it, 'hierohistory'. Likewise, a human being putting on a sacred animal mask in a certain ritual is not only taking on the form of an animal, but becoming that spirit, incorporating it before us on earth. This intermingling of worlds is essential to understanding Native American traditions, and fundamental to understanding the various cultures or 'artifacts'.

Frank Waters helps us understand better the concept of *kachinas* among the Hopi. He writes:

☙❧

The kachinas, then, are the inner forms, the spiritual components of the outer physical forms of life, which may be invoked to manifest their benign powers so that man may be enabled to continue his never-ending journey. They are the invisible forces of life – not gods, but rather intermediaries, messengers. Hence their chief function is to bring rain, insuring the abundance of crops and the continuation of life.[16]

☙❧

This means that those people who wear *kachina* masks and take on their powers, in turn have a grave responsibility to the tribe as a whole: they must not 'fall', commit indiscretions during this time, or otherwise imperil the continuation of traditional natural and spiritual cycles.

ABOVE *When a Plains Indian died, the body was often laid on a high platform for some days. Food and drink were offered to the dead person to strengthen their spirit.*

RIGHT *Tawa, the Kachina, or spirit-being, of the Sun.*

THE
ELEMENT
LIBRARY

NATIVE
AMERICAN
TRADITIONS

Waters describes not only what the *kachina* dancers look like during a ritual, but what they sing as well. He discusses their strange, other-worldly appearance, their toothy snouts and squash-blossom ears, their jewellery and their painted bodies, and then relates a song of the 'Long Hair' *kachinas*:

In the summertime we will come again. We will come as clouds from the west, the south, the east and the north to bless the Hopi people and to water their fields and crops. Then the Hopis will see their corn plants majestically growing. They will be so happy they will joyfully sing praises to the spirit-beings who brought moisture. At the edge of the cornfield a bird will sing with them in the oneness of their happiness. So they will sing together in tune with the universal power, in harmony with the creator of all things. And the bird song, and the people's song, and the song of life will become one.[17]

This is the best relation of human beings to spirit-beings: they exist in a natural harmony that is manifest in nature itself. The ceremonies of people augment and harmonize the natural order.

This is not to say that most indigenous American tribes practise what has been called by some anthropologists 'ancestor worship'. It is one thing to recognize that a holy person has become identified with a particular divine force; it is quite another to 'worship' one's ancestors as people, and one wonders really if this was ever practised by traditional peoples anywhere. Among many tribes, especially in North America, ancestors are regarded with reverence for the traditions they have transmitted, but may also be regarded with fear inasmuch as unresolved psychic forces may come back to haunt descendants. Among the Navajo, the Apache and numerous other tribes, a medicine man may be necessary to resolve such problems and restore harmony.

Religious leaders known as prophets appeared in Indian culture after the arrival of the whites. They predicted future events, urged their people to resist the onslaught of European ways of life and to return to traditional values. This is a prophet's lodge.

RECIPROCITY BETWEEN HUMANS AND THE SPIRIT WORLD

We mentioned earlier the world renewal ceremonies of the northern California tribes – which as we see here, have their parallels in Hopi tradition, as well as in many other Indian traditions. Underlying all such ceremonies is the fundamental recognition that human beings have a role to play in 'mediating' between the spirit world, the human world and the natural world, all of which are profoundly interrelated. Contrary to modern beliefs that man is nothing more than a biological machine within a larger machine of nature, according to these Native traditions human beings have an obligation to recognize, revere and even incarnate the spirit-beings who inform the natural realm. Human beings have an obligation to renew their connections to nature and to the divine realm, and this obligation is world renewal.

In traditional Native American cultures, there is a reciprocity between human beings and the spirit world based on gifts and gratitude. That is: people offer ritual gifts through spiritual practices, including dances, and in turn spirits bring gifts to the people. The greatest gifts, of course, are the continuation of beneficial weather conditions, good crops or good hunting and the thriving of the culture itself. Conversely, people give gifts to the spirit-beings, gifts that include fasting and other like practices, as well as sacrifices or offerings. All of these beliefs and rituals suggest a direct reciprocity between the other world and this one, people's response to which is gratitude and joy.

This reciprocity is reflected in some healing rituals as well. Wallace Black Elk, a contemporary Lakota Sioux shaman, tells how a young boy who didn't speak or move, was not responding to any hospital treatments. Indeed, the doctors could not even determine what was wrong with him. Wallace Black Elk was called in and performed a traditional healing ceremony in the hospital room, which he had shut into complete blackness. He performed certain ritual songs and in came Tunkashila, a manifestation of God 'shaped like a man', only glowing. Tunkashila said that the boy had been attacked by some power using the force of the spider web at the base of his brain. So Wallace Black Elk called in Iktomi, the red spider spirit, who removed the web from the boy and mysteriously left the sealed room with the gifts that had been brought. The boy was miraculously cured; not only was he able to eat and drink, but also to move around, although the hospital doctor was nonplussed, particularly about what he could possibly write in his medical report regarding spider spirits![18]

It was once common for Christian writers to claim that the spirit-beings who manifest in Native American rituals or traditions are really 'demons', but this rhetoric does nothing to explain cases like that just cited, nor is it fair to Native American traditions. On the other hand, it is said in many American Indian traditions that there are bad as well as good spirits, sorcerers as well as good medicine men like Wallace Black Elk who work for, 'health and help'. This perhaps parallels the Christian teaching that there are fallen as well as good angels, and certainly the recognition in cultures all around the world that there are destructive spirits and sorcerers who work with these spirits. But tribal peoples recognize, too, that those who engage in such practices pay the price, not only in this life, but in the afterlife as well.

RECIPROCITY BETWEEN
PHYSICAL LIFE AND THE AFTERLIFE

After a warrior had fallen in battle, his comrades danced for fifteen days in front of his tipi, proclaiming his great deeds and celebrating his noble death.

THE
ELEMENT
LIBRARY
NATIVE
AMERICAN
TRADITIONS

ABOVE *A gold funery mask from Peru. Such sumptuous masks were worn by the mummified corpses of the Sapa Incas during sacred ceremonies.*

ABOVE *A Chippewa widow with her dead husband's possessions, painted by the Canadian Indian artist Charlie Bird King c 1826.*

In many Native American traditions – as for northern European and other traditional indigenous peoples around the world – there is a reciprocity between this life and the afterlife. Among some prairie tribes it was held that scalping a vanquished enemy was not only a sign of one's physical triumph, but meant that one's enemy also became one's subordinate in the next life. And many peoples, including many American Indian tribes, hold that the dead ought to be furnished with certain symbolic goods that will accompany him into the next life. At the very least, this entails for instance a medicine bag, or other symbolic artifacts of his clan.

Among the Inca – and among some tribes in the south-eastern United States – this practice was taken to a grandiose extreme for the king or for royalty. The past emperors were mummified in Peruvian tradition, and during Inca sacred ceremonies were present on thrones, wearing gold masks and other magnificent jewellery, attended by waiting ladies and recognized as if they were present as they were in life. Indeed, it was expected that the emperor's retinue – his ladies in particular – would sacrifice themselves upon his death so as to accompany him into the afterlife[19]. Both practices – mummification and sacrifice of retinue – were based on the premise that this world and the afterlife are profoundly interrelated.

But there are other implications to such practices. Essentially, one has here the preservation of an individual's psyche in order to allow its purification in the afterlife, or to radiate its beneficent influences for the culture in the case of royalty identified with celestial powers. Soul purification is also found among the Sioux, and is one of their seven holy rites described by Black Elk in *The Sacred Pipe*. The Sioux 'keep a soul' in order to allow its purification after death, so that it can return directly to the Great Spirit rather than wandering in other afterlife states. A 'keeper of a soul' must be an extremely holy man; and the rites he keeps, are for the good of all the people as well as the individual soul.

In general, it is certainly fair to say that in American Indian traditions, much more than in modern European or American societies, both spirits and ancestors are revered for their gifts to us. This recognition is not a matter of 'cults of ancestor worship', but an awareness of the profound debt people of a tradition owe those from whom that tradition is inherited. What is more, recognizing spirits is not a matter of 'worshipping demons', but derives from a profound awareness of the interpenetrations of the spirit world, the afterlife, nature and the traditional human world. Even if modern people cannot accept these ideas, perhaps we can acknowledge what they signify for the Native peoples.

6

CEREMONIES AND RITUALS

All traditional cultures are drawn together by ritual or liturgical calendars that link the human, the natural, the celestial, and the divine realms. These rituals or ceremonies are astonishingly diverse, ranging from medieval Christian pageants to Australian Aboriginal dances, from Easter to solstice festivals. A similar diversity is obtained within American Indian traditions, ranging from the annual

Ritual dances formed a connection with the spirit world. The Buffalo Bull Dance of the Mandan tribe was performed to attract the spirit of the buffalo and call the herds closer to the hunters.

mask dances found in tribes on the east coast, the west coast and the southern United States down into Mesoamerica, to the Sun Dance of the Plains tribes, to the Midê ceremonies of the upper mid-west and Canada. However, regardless of this enormous range of rituals and ceremonies, we find the same traditional principles apply in all of them. This chapter examines these intermingled strands of ritual.

THE
ELEMENT
LIBRARY
NATIVE
AMERICAN
TRADITIONS

DANCE, DRUM AND SONG

ABOVE *An indoor ritual dance performed at Unalachet in Alaska.*

BELOW *Another version of the many Buffalo Dances created by the Plains Indians to ensure a successful buffalo hunt.*

It is said that many Native American traditions are traditions of dance and of the drum. And indeed, although there are countless kinds of dances across the Americas, they do share a fundamental symbolism, and allow for the intertribal pow-wows, or dances, now common across the United States. There are some tribes whose members often dance deosil, or clockwise, and others who dance widdershins, or counterclockwise, but in either case they move around a centre and, unlike European ballet, which often seems to be a leaping up away from the earth, tribal dancers seem to move their feet downward to greet the earth. A dancer will tell you that he feels the dance within him through the drum.

The drum in many Native American traditions forms a connection to the spirit world, so much so that some traditions even speak of a 'drum religion'. In Eskimo shamanism, the medicine man drums until the spirits come in and speak through him, in a kind of possession. Sometimes this possession is an 'acting out' of, or identification with, an inward drama, and sometimes it is an actual possession; but in either case the drum itself forges a connection between the spirits and this world. The same is true, although in a perhaps less overt way, in the more southern traditions as well.

Along with dancing and drumming, tribal traditions also include chants or songs. These songs are in some cases continuations of mythological cycles, recitations of 'events' that take place in a visionary or super-historical world. In other cases the songs are invocations of particular helping spirits, or of the Great Spirit. But in any event, these songs are often an expression of gratitude for what has been given us human beings. Generally simple on the surface, songs or chants are nonetheless part of a liturgical cycle of great complexity and intricate symbolism that reveals humanity completely interlinked with nature, the sky, and the spirits.

RITUAL CYCLES

The great liturgical or ritual cycles of the American Indian tribes are, like those of the other world religions, profoundly bound up with the annual cycles of the seasons. The annual ceremonial cycles, whether for hunting societies or for agricultural societies, always seek to affirm and augment proper natural conditions: the rituals seek to balance or even to intensify the conditions necessary for much game or for good crops. Ceremonies mark spring and winter, especially; and indeed, a number of ritual sites in the Americas mark the solstices or equinoxes with precise alignments. Even though we no longer know the exact ceremonies for which these sites were made, still in their alignments we see how precisely astrological knowledge informed tribal rituals.[20]

The tribal traditions also include divisions marking the individual life cycle. Birth, puberty, maturity, death, are marked in virtually all traditions by special rituals that are often directly linked to the annual or cosmic cycles. Hence, a birth might well be celebrated in the spring because of the affiliated celestial and seasonal symbolism of rebirth. Initiations are often linked to the annual cycles, an initiation signifying a rebirth; and individual life cycles do not take place in isolation from the greater tribal or annual liturgical or ritual cycles, for all form an interconnected unity.

Hence many tribes celebrate a New Year festival that represents on earth the birth of

the people and of the cosmos itself. This festival is essentially a world renewal festival which marks the revitalization of the natural and human worlds. It is often marked in part by reverence for the ancestors, but in any case, it represents the return of the world from bleakness to fertility or vitality. The New Year is a call for renewed abundant crops, for renewed health among the people, for the blessings of the spirits upon the earth. In many tribes, the New Year festival is the recounting of the original creation, which is not merely a static creation 'event' in linear historical time, but a manifestation of divine forces in this present moment.

TOP *Ritual dancing is being performed once again by American Indians. Some traditions and rituals have been lost forever, but many have been rediscovered. This is the Elk Medicine Dance.*

ABOVE *Pueblo Indians dressed for the Corn Dance. As settled farmers, the Pueblo performed dances in all seasons of the year to ensure the good growth of crops.*

THE CEREMONY OF THE SWEAT LODGE

A similar significance appears in the ceremony of the sweat lodge practised by the Plains tribes. In this case, the lodge represents a rebirth or purification for the individual, and a microcosm, or image of the cosmos. A sweat lodge is an enclosed space, sometimes half sunk into the earth, but always directionally oriented, into which the

medicine man brings heated rocks — representing primordial creation itself — and adds holy water to them, so that inside the lodge becomes hot and steamy. Those who go into the sweat lodge purify themselves by entering into this primordial microcosm, composed of the primal elements: earth (including stone and wood), fire, air, water.

THE
ELEMENT
LIBRARY
NATIVE
AMERICAN
TRADITIONS

Black Elk explains this symbolism of rebirth in more detail:

∽∽

The sweat lodge is made of from twelve to sixteen young willows, and these, too, have a lesson to teach us, for in the fall their leaves die and return to the earth, but in the spring they come to life again. So too, men die, but live again in the real world of Wakan-Tanka, where there is nothing but the spirits of all things, and this true life we may know here on earth if we purify our bodies and minds, thus coming closer to Wakan-Tanka, who is all-purity.[21]

∽∽

From this brief description of only one aspect of the ceremony, we can see that everything in it has a special significance – from the darkness of the lodge, representing human ignorance, to the four openings of the sacred door, signifying the four ages – reminding participants of their need to be purified and to be humble before the sacred

powers of the directions and before the Creator Himself. From this ceremony, Black Elk tells us, the tribal people used to gain their spiritual power and, he says, he cries now when he thinks of how little his people still hold to such ceremonies.

It is true that not all tribes have sweat lodges per se; but a similar symbolism appears in the sacred lodges of many tribes, including the Iroquois and the Ojibway, the Creek and other south-eastern tribes. Some eastern tribes have what is called the 'great lodge', which like the sweat lodge embodies directional symbolism, and incorporates other microcosmic symbolism as well. This is also true of the Midê lodges of the upper mid-west, and of the *kivas* of the Pueblo peoples. While the rites concerned vary enormously, their symbolism – the way in which the lodges mirror the cosmos as a whole – is fundamentally similar right across the Americas.

BELOW *Warriors had to learn to suffer hardship and pain with fortitude and stoicism. To do this, they would regularly test their mettle with self-imposed torture. Here Mandan men undergo a form of the Sun Dance.*

THE SUN DANCE

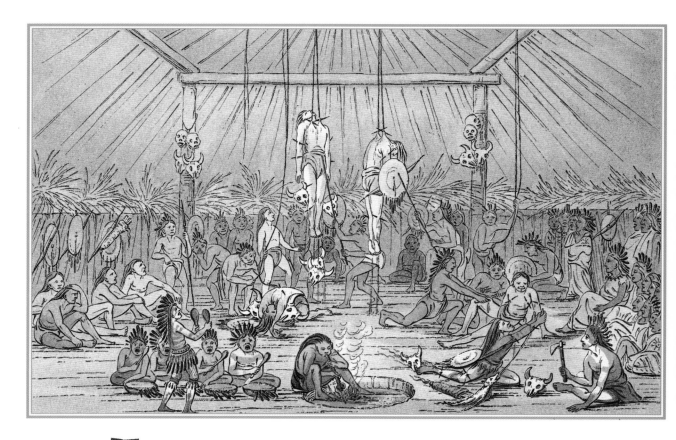

Although much has been written about it, we should also discuss another ceremony that, although it is celebrated by the Plains tribes, reveals certain symbolisms found in different forms among virtually all the Native American traditions, and that is certainly important to recognize on its own account as well: the Sun Dance. The Sun Dance exemplifies the symbolism that we spoke of earlier regarding the sacred dances and chants of many tribes. In the Sun Dance ceremony, held annually in the summer, a central pole is erected, representing the world axis, atop which is attached a buffalo skull. As with the sweat lodge, so everything in the sacred geography of the Sun Dance is significant and aligned directionally on an east-west axis, including the drum and the sacred fire as well as the respective positions of dance sponsor and the medicine man chief.

The Sun Dance is based on the concept of sacrifice, just as are rituals in many other world religions, including Vedic tradition, Judaism and Christianity, for example. In earlier times, the Sun Dance entailed warriors driving skewers through their chest muscles, skewers tied to the central pole, physically manifesting the linking of the heart to the cosmic axis. Dancers would dance, linked thus, until their skewers pulled free from their chests. In more recent times, this practice has been discontinued, but participants still go through a ceremonial ordeal, fasting from food and water, and hence the principles – sacrifice and the linking of the dancers and the central pole – are continued still.

Thomas Yellowtail, Sun Dance chief of the Crow tribe, elaborates on the symbolism of the Sun Dance:

ABOVE *A Sioux warrior in the Sun Ritual Stance, riding bareback to greet the sun.*

◎◎

As the drum beats, it establishes the heartbeat for the dancers, our tribe, and all of mankind. We feel this link in our hearts, and when the drum gives its call and the dancers respond by blowing their eagle bone whistles, we reach into our innermost centre, and blessings penetrate all those present at the same time that our prayers rise up to all the universe.[22]

◎◎

What is more, he continues, although there is no physical connection between the dancers and the pole, 'the Centre Pole contains all of the sacred power of the universe', and the dancers are each 'connected to the Centre Pole by an invisible cord coming from the tree and penetrating into their heart'.[23]

We should probably emphasize here that ceremonies like the Sun Dance are seen to have a significance, not only for the individual and the tribe, but for the entire cosmos as well. Like the Greek Orthodox Liturgy of St John Chrysostom, the American Indian liturgy here calls upon the Creator to bless the participants, the countryside, the government, and the whole world. In other words, such ceremonies are recognized as a means of manifesting blessings and harmony on earth. This requires and is based in sacrifice: just as Christians are called to follow Christ's path, so too the Plains people follow the Sun Dance way, which is the way of sacrifice and, in the words of the Sioux, Fools Crow 'the highest expression of our religion'.

THE
ELEMENT
LIBRARY
NATIVE
AMERICAN
TRADITIONS

CEREMONIES AND RITUALS UNDER THREAT

Apache Indians dressed as Devil Dancers. Some of the interest in revived traditions is fuelled by the tourist trade and many 'rituals' may be less than authentic.

Unfortunately, many tribal ceremonies have been lost since the nineteenth century, losses that have come in large part because of the erosive power of the modern world. For some time, tribal rituals were actually made illegal in the United States – including, incredibly, even the tradition of the 'giveaway', according to which one's nobility was measured by what one gave away to others – and had to be carried on in secret. This secrecy in turn meant that sometimes normal generational transmission did not happen, and hence some ceremonies can no longer be properly performed. Indeed, sometimes one finds young tribal people searching records and trying to reconstruct some rituals as closely as possible. But many ceremonies have been irretrievably lost.

In addition, the ritual cycles and connections to many sacred sites have also been lost. There are sacred sites across the United States that – because the tribes have been dislocated, moved sometimes nearly a thousand miles away – are no longer part of the annual cycle that once linked man, nature, and the spirits through a liturgical and mythological tradition bound to special sacred places. These sites once had myths affiliated to them, myths that represented links to the celestial world, and these myths, along with the religious rites that accompanied them, cannot be fully retrieved or reconstructed.

Thomas Yellowtail addresses such losses when speaking to Indian peoples generally. He says that there is no use in mourning rituals now lost, or in wishing that one could reconstruct them through human effort alone. Rather, he asserts, tribal people should concentrate on the ceremonies that remain, trying to preserve them as perfectly as possible. He tells us:

⊚⊚

Modern Indians care little for spiritual things and traditional ways, so there are very few traditional people remaining with real medicine or understanding. Modern civilization has no understanding of sacred matters. Everything is backwards. This makes it even more important that young people follow what is left today. Even though many of the sacred ways are no longer with us, what we have left is enough for anyone, and if it is followed, it will lead as far as the person can go.[24]

⊚⊚

The traditional ways must be preserved for the next generation, he urges; for, according to tribal ways, ritual is central to the tribe's continuation. Modern people seem to think that ceremonies are but entertainment – a view reinforced by intertribal 'show dancing' for tourists – or mere 'superstition'. But in fact rituals are the form, the crystallization, of the mythological and religious cycles that not only make sense of the cosmos, but in fact reveal, augment, and even bring about human beings' harmony with it. Without ritual, the tribal tradition has no formal expression, and ceases to exist except as a matter of bloodline and transmitted stories. For traditional culture – art, tools, clothing, even weapons – derives from and reflects its ceremonial centre, that in turn emerges from the revealed religion itself.

7

SHAMANISM AND MEDICINE

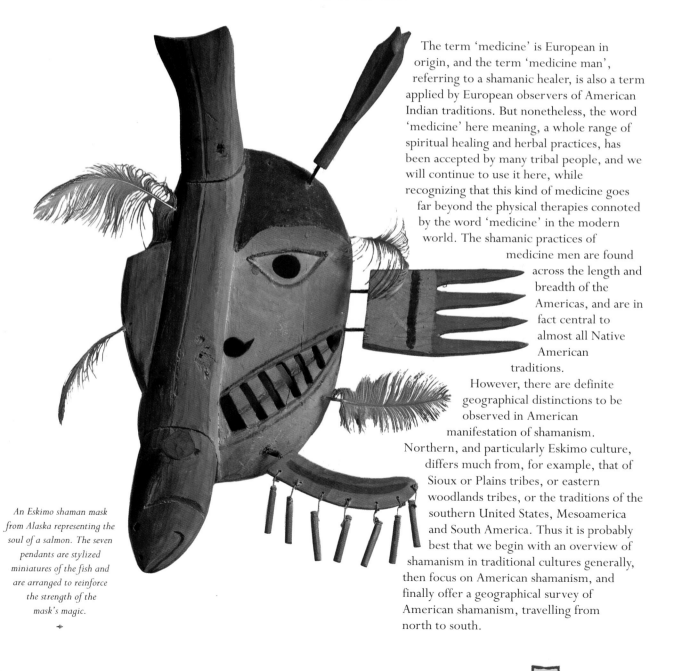

The term 'medicine' is European in origin, and the term 'medicine man', referring to a shamanic healer, is also a term applied by European observers of American Indian traditions. But nonetheless, the word 'medicine' here meaning, a whole range of spiritual healing and herbal practices, has been accepted by many tribal people, and we will continue to use it here, while recognizing that this kind of medicine goes far beyond the physical therapies connoted by the word 'medicine' in the modern world. The shamanic practices of medicine men are found across the length and breadth of the Americas, and are in fact central to almost all Native American traditions.

However, there are definite geographical distinctions to be observed in American manifestation of shamanism. Northern, and particularly Eskimo culture, differs much from, for example, that of Sioux or Plains tribes, or eastern woodlands tribes, or the traditions of the southern United States, Mesoamerica and South America. Thus it is probably best that we begin with an overview of shamanism in traditional cultures generally, then focus on American shamanism, and finally offer a geographical survey of American shamanism, travelling from north to south.

An Eskimo shaman mask from Alaska representing the soul of a salmon. The seven pendants are stylized miniatures of the fish and are arranged to reinforce the strength of the mask's magic.

THE
ELEMENT
LIBRARY
NATIVE
AMERICAN
TRADITIONS

Shamanism - an overview

Shamanism is essentially indigenous visionary spirituality. The shaman either undergoes a visionary journey through the cosmos, or calls spirits to him, in order to heal or to accomplish other benefits for the tribal people who he represents. Shamanism appears in many forms, and geographically is found all the way from central Asia and Siberia through Alaska and Canada, as well as in the United States and South America. Similar traditional practices are also found in Australia, Africa and Europe. A shaman is, in general, 'called' by the spirits to his vocation, and is then initiated into the shamanic tradition by a practising shaman.

Shamanism is in many ways the most primordial of all religious traditions; it is certainly the most archaic of traditions, and in some ways the most dangerous as well. For the shaman must either undertake arduous journeys of the spirit, sometimes through very hostile realms, on behalf of others; or he must work with spirits, among whom he must be able to differentiate, and from whom his protection is both his tradition and his spiritual power, or his spiritual protectors. Shamanism, while it engages the psyche at levels unfamiliar to most of us, is not merely a matter of psychology.

Although there are some modern authors who give workshops on shamanism, and although there are some popular novelists who have written extensively on quasi-shamans, one must be quite careful in this realm. To be a shaman is not merely a weekend of entertainment, at least not in any traditional culture. Rather, it is a very powerful and dangerous practice to which one is called, at times even against one's own desires, in order to work on behalf of one's tribe. One can certainly contact powerful and archaic images in the psyche; but this is not the same as shamanism seen in toto, which entails a total cosmology,[25] and sometimes contact with very hostile discarnate entities.

The medicine man of the tribe had to diagnose sickness, collect the necessary remedial herbs and prepare them himself, using incantations and prayers as he worked.

NORTH AMERICAN SHAMANISM

The most well-known North American shamanism is probably that of the Eskimo tribes of Alaska, and the tribes of northern Canada. That the North American forms of shamanism are related to the shamanism of Siberia, central Asia, and perhaps Europe, is virtually certain, although precisely what this relationship means is presently unclear. Some theorize that shamanism travelled from Siberia to the Americas, but there is no way, as yet, to demonstrate this conclusively. Nonetheless, Eskimo shamanism reveals the same fundamental symbolism found in Shamanism practised in Siberia.

Eskimo Shamanism

The symbolic pattern of Eskimo shamanism is like that of shamanism in general. The would-be shaman receives a 'call' to his vocation, withdraws into solitude away from society, undertakes apprenticeship to a master, undergoes an initiatic death and resurrection, acquires one or more familiar spirits, and learns the 'secret language' of nature and the spirits. He becomes able to undergo ecstatic flights of the soul on behalf of others, and travels through realms of the cosmos inaccessible to others. Finally, he becomes a fully-fledged healer and practising shaman in the culture, a figure earning respect, fear, and even awe, as well as gratitude.[26]

Earlier, we described a shamanic journey among the Eskimo, and how in particular the shaman, or *angakuk*, while tied and restrained in the presence of tribal people, may 'travel' down under the sea or up into the heavens on behalf of some people or person.[27] Sometimes it is a matter of recovering a 'lost soul', while at other times it is a matter of finding out what taboos have been broken, in order that recompense can be made. For instance, the shaman might find in the visionary realm that seals were not coming to the tribe because some members had broken several taboos, and they need to put this right.

The Eskimo cosmology includes a celestial world above and an underworld below. When the shaman 'travels' to the sky realm – the happy celestial abode of the dead – he often does so for sheer joy, or in order to speak with and learn from the ancestors who now dwell in the sky realm. The sky realm is a world of peace, in which the dead remain happy, and the primary difference from our world is the 'reversal' of things there. Winter here is summer there, and so forth. Below our world is the underworld, to which those who are punished in the afterlife go; it is rather like the classical Greek Hades.

Shamanism is a distinct vocation, connected, in part, to secret societies, and always to a master–disciple initiation, but it should be added that shamanism is found throughout a tribe in more individualized ways. For instance, non-shaman members of northern American or Eskimo tribes may practise divination rituals themselves, and have a guardian spirit and other aspects of shamanism in their daily lives. However, the shaman has more of this power in his life; he is more experienced, possesses more guardian spirits, is initiated, and in general has more knowledge of, and power in, non-physical realms than the average person.

Ojibway Shamanism

This same permeation of shamanism through a tribe is found in the Midêwiwin or Midê lodges, or secret societies, of the Ojibway in Canada and the upper United States. That is: many members of the tribe may belong to the Midê secret society, at least at a basic level, but progressively fewer are members of the Midê higher levels. The idea of participation in the same realities for all members of the tribe remains; but again, there are degrees of power or participation, and shamans form the highest level – they are the healers and performers of miracles.

There are divisions of shamans in the Midê: one has on the one hand the *jossakid,* and on the other the *wabeno.* The *jossakid* are perhaps better known; they are the 'jugglers' who, like the Eskimo *angakuk,* are miraculously

As important as the tribes chief, the Medicine Man of the nomadic Plains Indians presided over the break-up of encampments and lead his tribe to a suitable new site.

freed of their bonds by the spirits, untied in darkness and solitude in an instant. The *jossakid* are also responsible for the 'shaking tent', a ceremony in which the veiled shaman does battle with spirits, or undertakes spiritual journeys hidden in an enclosure or behind a veil; the *jossakid* perform healing. The *wabeno*, or 'men of dawn' are known for their 'fire handling', their touching of live coals, and many other mysterious abilities, based upon fire.

According to Mircea Eliade, the Midê lodges and other secret shamanic societies were established in order to eliminate or obviate sorcery or black magic, which by definition is self-seeking and unconnected to or deviating from a religious tradition.[28] Thus the Midê represent a movement back towards

THE
ELEMENT
LIBRARY
NATIVE
AMERICAN
TRADITIONS

ABOVE *Healing was a matter of spiritual as well as medicinal treatment. A Tlinkit shaman makes incantations to the spirits to drive away his patient's illness.*

ABOVE *In the 1990s, the interest in the healing connection between the mind and body is growing stronger in the west. Modern medicine men such as Rolling Thunder, shown above, are demonstrating their skills.*

a pure or primordial tradition, and for this reason we find in them an emphasis on the celestial realm, and on rebirth through initiation, on which in fact the entire concept of Midêwiwin depends. According to Midê mythology, Manabôzhô, the divine messenger of the Great Spirit, gave to enfeebled mankind in this degenerate time the spiritual power represented in the otterspirit, in order to show him the right way to live.

This otter mythology makes symbolic sense. For the otter moves gracefully between the waters and the earth, just as the shaman moves gracefully from one realm to another. And so too, the otter symbol, represented in the otter medicine pouch, reigns over the mysteries of the Midê lodge. Although we will discuss this in detail later, suffice it to say here that the otter represents one of the animal totems under whose guidance the lodge operates; it represents a guiding or protecting spirit. The otter pouch contains *mîgîs* shells, sacred shells representing spiritual power.

In these *mîgîs* shells there is a great mystery. Like certain traditions among the Australian Aborigine shamans, the initiatory rebirth of the Midê neophyte consists in having certain sacred *mîgîs* shells 'shot' into the body, especially at the joints and the heart. In this 'shooting' ceremony, the initiate falls down unconscious, and is finally raised up again by means of the sacred pouch, but as a reborn and initiated man, one with spiritual power. When he falls down he is 'killed', and so he has undergone death and rebirth.

Before this rebirth takes place, the initiate has already been taught the symbolism of the drum and how to exorcize bad spirits, as well as magical songs and herbal plant powers; he has been purified in the sweat lodge many times and, most of all, has learnt ritual songs and spiritual doctrines. In other words, the initiate has been purified and has come to embody in himself as much as is possible the tradition and its ramifications.

Traditionally, there are four levels of this initiation process, but each is a repetition and intensification of the last; at the end of all four levels, the initiate will be acknowledged as a fully-fledged shaman.

Winnebago Shamanism

The Winnebago, a tribe of the northern United States, also have a shamanic initiatory tradition, called the Medicine Rite. This entails the symbolic death and resurrection of the initiate by means of an otterskin pouch. This symbolism of rebirth is reiterated by the image of the child, which the initiate symbolically becomes after being reborn: once one is born anew, one grows up anew into shamanic adulthood. The initiate is given the secrets of the afterlife and of entering into the eternal presence of Creation.

Parallels with Aztec Ceremonies

Some authors speculate that there is a pan-American shamanist origin for the secret orders or brotherhoods like the Midê and Winnebago Medicine Society, which is reflected also in such tribes as the Pawnee, and some other Plains tribes, down into Mexico. Certainly, there are striking ceremonial parallels between many of these tribes and Aztec ceremonies. One Pawnee ceremony with definite Aztec connections, discontinued in the nineteenth century, entailed the sacrifice of a virgin girl by shooting her with a sacred arrow. Pawnee ceremonies of shamanic initiation also reveal similarities to the Aztec rituals.

Interestingly, Mircea Eliade interprets the Ghost Dance religion that swept many American tribes during the late nineteenth century as a kind of widespread shamanism – 'democratized shamanism', as it were – which represents the purest form of 'return to origins', inasmuch as there isn't even an initiatory structure in the Ghost Dance religion. Rather, anyone who participated might be touched with the eagle feather, fall down 'dead', visit the spirits of the dead and be revived again. Indeed, there were even cases of people being resuscitated from death through the Ghost Dance, which Eliade calls a return, at the end of time, to time's beginning – a return to the 'eternal now' and the Golden Age.[29]

SOUTH AMERICAN SHAMANISM

Although it is dangerous to make generalizations about the shamanism of an entire continent, nonetheless, one can safely say that while South American shamanism manifests virtually all the characteristics of Northern American shamanism, including the visionary journeys, the calling of spirits, and initiation rites, South American shamanism is in a sense more colourful than its northern counterparts. That is, it is closely linked to the whole complex of mythological and cosmological symbolism manifested in the rich art and architecture of Mesoamerica and South America, and includes certain aspects – theriomorphic transformations like were-cats, for instance – not usually found in the north.

It is no longer possible to determine precisely what role shamanism played in the great civilizations of South America now gone; but one can see parallels or connections between the great priesthoods and the shamanic traditions, particularly in so far as mythology is concerned. But we can only speak with some certainty about the Indian tribes that still exist and that, as we suggested in our first chapter, maintain in more or less popular forms some aspects of the earlier civilizations. One suspects, however, that shamanism as we see it in the many scattered tribes of Mesoamerica and South America – and in North America and elsewhere – is of enormous antiquity, predating all the great civilizations. In its present forms, shamanism is scattered, if widespread, and the reader will therefore forgive me for making general comments about South American shamanism.

Soul Loss

One characteristic shared with much of Siberian shamanism – and also with some northern American shamanism – is a belief in soul loss. Many South American tribes hold that through illness or sorcery, a human might 'lose his soul', meaning that the psyche, or an element of it, is no longer integrated with the entire being, and the shaman must search for it in the psychic realms and bring it back. Allied to this idea of the shaman as a celestial guide, is the belief that he ought to guide the soul of a person newly dead to the realm of the sky. It is a difficult journey, which the shaman knows well, and can accomplish much more quickly and easily than the abandoned soul who has just left the physical realm.

The Shaman as Intermediary Between the Tribe and the Divine

There are other traditions among South American tribes that parallel Siberian shamanism, chief among which is how the shaman or shamaness acts as the intermediary between the tribe and the Divine. This same symbolism is found in the priesthoods of organized religious traditions such as the Aztec; but in the tribal shamanic symbolism it is starkly present: the shamaness or *machi* goes on to a hill, goes into a trance, 'travels' to the Sky Father, importunes him, comes back to the people, and announces to them what she has learnt by way of the visionary journey.[30] In the course of this journey – like Siberian shamans – she may well have to fight demons, the story of which she also recounts to the tribe.

An Oyrots shaman from Russia preparing for the horse sacrifice. The drum is used to summon the horse's spirit. Siberian shamanism has much in common with South American Shamanism.

THE
ELEMENT
LIBRARY
NATIVE
AMERICAN
TRADITIONS

The Shaman as Healer

Above all, however, South American shamanism entails healing, in particular what is known as 'object extraction'. The shaman 'sucks out' of the patient's body foreign objects that may have been introduced by spirits or sorcerers and that cause an illness. Sometimes the shaman also sucks out ' bad blood', but in any case, the ailing patient is cured through the opening up of the body – sometimes to the point of exposing entrails – and the removal of imbalance or evil. As many observers have pointed out, this 'object extraction' has parallels in northern traditions, and reflects the archaic symbolism of rebirth, of the creation of a virtual 'new body' through initiation.

Fire and Heat

A final characteristic of South American shamanism we will consider is the importance of fire and heat. There are many fiery magical events in South American shamanism, including handling or walking over fiery coals,

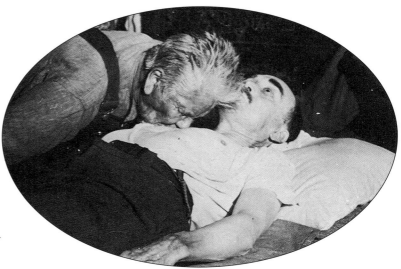

as well as the 'heating' of the shaman himself, which marks certain degrees of yogic attainment in both Hinduism and Tibetan Buddhism as well. All of these phenomena mark the shaman's transfer into other realms and, while these practices may violate contemporary beliefs regarding the 'laws of physics', this is only because modern, materialistic views limit themselves to the physical realm in the cosmos, and ignore all other possibilities.

ABOVE *Many shamans were believed to have power over death itself. Here, a Chippewa Sucking Doctor tries to revive his patient.*

LEFT *Preventative medicine was an established concept in Indian culture. Here, a Navajo medicine man performs a female shoot chant for a mother and her baby to promote good health.*

PARALLELS IN
WORLDWIDE SHAMANISM

In conclusion, we might look at the
remarkable parallels between different forms
of shamanism around the world. Many
scholars have suggested actual contact
between shamanic cultures as diverse as the
Laplander, the South American, the North
American, the Siberian, the Australian, the
Far Eastern, and other groups. It may well be
that there was 'cultural diffusion' in antiquity;
one can hardly doubt it. However, there is
another possible explanation for the
remarkable unanimity of apparently unrelated
cultures regarding such things as initiations,
cosmology, medical practices, artistic images,
ritual songs, and 'magical phenomena'.

These shamanic traditions may all simply
reflect actual human experiences. It could be
that there are realms in the cosmos other than
the physical on which modern scientific
attention is so relentlessly focused, and that
people may indeed contact or enter those
realms. One enters those realms in similar

LEFT *A Zulu witch
doctor practising as an
oracle to predict the
future and interpret
the present.*

BELOW *The tools of the
trade carried by an
Ashanti Medicine Man in
Africa bear an affinity
with those used by the
Native American
shamans.*

ways. Such a possibility is of course
uncomfortable for us, not least since it
suggests that far from knowing everything
about the cosmos, we in fact know very little.
Whatever the truths the unanimity of
shamanism on certain matters or practices
does suggest that we too have something to
learn from it, and that we may well ignore it
at our cost. At the very least, we ought to
recognize and respect this, our common
archaic human inheritance.

8

TOTEMS

Many aboriginal cultures, including the American Indian traditions, recognize a much deeper connection between people and animals than modern people do. Indeed, many American Indian cultures are organized precisely by 'clans', societal groups under the sign or totem of an animal. Examples of totemic animals include deer, elk, otters and eagles. This is no accidental or superficial relationship. Underlying this clan structure is a fundamental recognition of the profound spiritual relationships that exist between human beings, nature, and the subtle and archetypal worlds. In brief: the natural behaviour that was once denigrated by anthropologists from the west as 'totem worship' is in fact a profound recognition of traditional Indian cosmology, and of how both humanity and nature reflect their subtle and spiritual origins.

Totems representing the clan or family outside houses at Alert Bay, British Columbia.

THE THREE WORLDS

To begin with, we should note that traditionally, in American Indian as in Platonic and other traditional cosmologies, there are 'three worlds': the physical, the subtle and the spiritual. In all these traditions, the physical world is animated by the subtle realm, which in turn reflects its spiritual origin. To give an example: an eagle we see in the sky is animated by its subtle being, bodying forth the archetype of eagle, an eternal archetype of the golden, soaring, solar bird; it is also an entrypoint into the transcendent. An eagle, therefore, can be seen to exist on three levels at once. This is also true of human beings.

Understanding these 'three worlds' is critical to understanding not only Native American traditions generally, but totemic symbolism in particular. As we noted earlier, this multiple world concept helps us understand such Indian traditions as masks and dances, for these in turn reflect the subtle world and the spiritual world in artistic form. Central to these cultural forms is the concept of the three worlds that also naturally informs the totemic traditions. For the totems – which are in fact archetypal forms – reveal powers in the subtle world and have their manifestations in the physical world.

Scholar Ake Hultkranz has noted the controversy between academic specialists in totemic symbolism, some of whom argue that totems represent archetypes, while others argue that totems are not to be worshipped, but possess primarily cultural or semiotic significance.[31] The answer to this dilemma probably lies in this doctrine of three worlds. The totem's ultimate significance derives from its spiritual origin, while its meaning in the natural world derives from its archetypal significance in the subtle world, or realm of souls. One does not worship the totem itself any more than the Green Orthodox person worships the form of an icon – one reveres what the icon or totem signifies, as an aspect of the Divine itself. Cultural significances of totems are reflections or reverberations of this symbolism.

In other words, in its essence a totem manifests a spiritual form or truth – as aspect of the Divine – and the totem's cultural meanings derive from or reflect this truth. To have as one's totem the bear, for example, may or may not mean that one is prohibited from killing actual bear. But it does probably mean that one's cultural artifacts will reflect this symbolism, either in a medicine pouch, or in forms on clothing, or other signs that act as reminders and invocations of the bear's spiritual power and protection. It also means that if one is a member of the bear clan, one will not marry another member of that clan, a largely inflexible tribal prohibition.

From this prohibition against intraclan marriage, we can see a connection between the totem and ancestors which is emphasized in some tribes. Some tribes (like the Arawak in South America and the Yuchi in the south-eastern United States) affirm that tribal people have their origin in the manifestation

To contact the spirit world, medicine men had to efface their own shape and personality. Here a Blackfoot medicine man is completely transformed by a huge yellow bear skin. He carries a medicine spear to ward off evil spirits.

THE
ELEMENT
LIBRARY
NATIVE
AMERICAN
TRADITIONS

of certain animal spirit-beings, another way of expressing how the human world is connected to, and derives from, the archetypal realm. Thus the individual clans are reminders of the world's archetypal origin and significance – and in particular, of our human archetypal origin and meaning. Other tribes believe that in mythological 'hierohistory', the Creator sent archetypal 'helping spirits' to tribal people, rather than saying that tribes are directly derived from archetypal animal spirits. But the significance of these myths connecting human beings to the archetypal realm remains similar.

Clans and totems reveal to us once again how profoundly Native American traditions embody a unity between the human, the natural, and the spirit realms. Totemic symbolism and clan structure show how the human and the natural worlds are interrelated, in that both 'descend from' and manifest common spiritual origins. One may say that the totem itself exists in the timeless archetypal world, but is embodied on the one hand in nature, manifesting especially strongly in certain animals, and on the other hand in the human world, not only in clans, but in cultural artifacts like clothing, pouches and symbolic carvings or even petroglyphs etched in stone. The totem exists above and beyond time, but manifests in time, in both human and natural worlds.

THE GUARDIAN SPIRIT

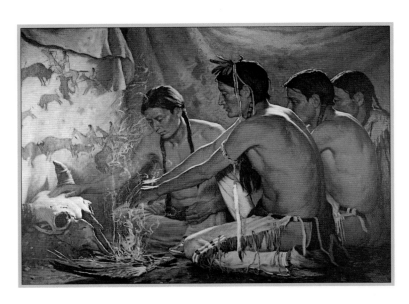

Young hunters gather inside their lodge to offer prayers to the spirit of the Buffalo. Sage is burnt to cleanse and purify the hunters.

It is not surprising that totemic symbolism is closely related to that of the individual guardian spirit. In some tribes (particularly in Mesoamerica and South America) this guardian spirit is recognized as being affiliated with an individual from birth, while in other tribes it is seen as being 'acquired' or, perhaps more accurately, revealed through ascetic practices like fasting in wilderness isolation. What is more, in some cases, the guardian spirit is regarded as naturally being of the totem spirit in one's clan – a bear or otter spirit, for example. All of this suggests that under consideration here is a kind of archetypal 'hierohistory' of a human being, a revelation both in the case of the totem and in the guardian spirit, of the human being's timeless archetypal counterpart or aspect.

Without question, the clearest manifestation of this archetypal relationship is to be seen in the Mesoamerican and South American traditions that refer to the *nagual*, or totemic spiritual guardian from birth. From an Aztec word meaning 'masked', *nagual* refers to the animal guardian spirit or ally that everyone in the tribe has, but that shamans have much more strongly or intensely. Indeed, it is said that some shamans can actually transform into their *nagual* form, and hence sometimes a shaman's enemies will try to kill animals of his totem, in the hope of killing the one into which the shaman is temporarily transformed, or to which he is intimately related.

Such a relationship between an individual and his guardian spirit is not restricted to the southern tribes, however; it is found right across the Americas, in the United States from Maine to the Plains, to the far western tribes. There is the widespread belief that a shaman can transform himself into his totemic ally; and widespread, too, is the belief that if the totemic animal is wounded or killed, so too will be the shaman in human form. While the guardian spirit is more intimately related to the natural world and its symbolism than the Christian concept of the guardian angel, much of the same symbolism does apply in the American Indian traditions, the guardian spirits often warn against bad actions and protect one from harm.

The guardian spirit, or totem, is often symbolized by a medicine bundle. A bundle

contains various 'relics', or special consecrated objects revealing the interconnected cosmological nexus associated with one's particular animal spirit. A medicine bundle or pouch is sacred, its contents not meant to be divulged. Among some tribes, including the Blackfoot, one might receive a bundle from someone else, and for this one gives a remuneration. Among other tribes, the bundle or medicine pouch is not transferred. But in all cases, the bundle marks the unique relationship one has with a guardian spirit or totem.

Although all Indians endeavoured to communicate with the spirit world, the shaman was better prepared to receive great visions. Here, a Sioux shaman attunes himself to the world beyond the physical.

VISION SEEKING

It is interesting that, while for tribes west of the Rocky Mountains, guardian spirit visions are not so much sought as come unasked, while many tribes east of the Rockies emphasize vision seeking. Black Elk, the great Lakota Sioux visionary, described how one traditionally 'laments for a vision':

Every man can cry for a vision, or 'lament'; and in the old days we all — men and women — 'lamented' all the time. What is received through the 'lamenting' is determined in part by the character of the person who does this, for it is only those people who are very qualified who receive the great visions, which are interpreted by our holy man, and which give strength and insight to our nation. It is very important for a person who wishes to 'lament' to receive aid and advice from a wicasa wakan (holy man) so that everything is done correctly, for if things are not done in the right way, something very bad can happen, and even a serpent could come and wrap itself around the 'lamenter'.[32]

In other words, to seek a vision is a very serious matter, and if there are differences between tribes as to whether visions are sought or come unsought, the tribes are nonetheless in agreement that a great vision comes only to those able to receive it, and that the traditional ways must be observed.

To seek a vision is indeed a serious thing, and for those tribes whose traditions entail

THE
ELEMENT
LIBRARY
NATIVE
AMERICAN
TRADITIONS

vision seeking there is necessarily a ritual to be followed in doing so. Certainly vision seeking is not merely a matter of running off to the wilderness and staying in solitude. Rather, the ritual, as Black Elk describes it, entails first of all seeking the guidance of a qualified holy man. From him one receives

instruction in the rituals to follow, which include offerings, the building of a purification or sweat lodge, the conducting of a special sweat lodge ceremony, special blessing and retirement to a high place, often a mountain, after which one stays in a ritually consecrated area and follows the guidance of the holy man.[33]

A successful vision-seeking might entail a sacred dream with special meaning, or it might entail the appearance of a sacred spirit who has an animal form, or a

Old Bear, a Mandan shaman, in full regalia, with rattles to call up the spirits, special headdress and face painted for ritual.

theriomorphic human form, forms like those seen on South American carvings or art works for instance, with human and animal characteristics together. This spirit bestows the special medicine power that is his to offer, and also gives the medicine song to summon the power or spirit. Finally, the spirit may detail the contents of the sacred bundle that the visionary is to have, which might include certain animal parts, certain plants, or other symbolic objects. After the visionary experience, the visionary might wear sacred forms he has seen, and designs on his body or clothing that also call in this sacred power.

Here again we see the 'three worlds' of which we have been speaking throughout this discussion. That is, through fasting and other ascetic practices and purifications, the vision seeker is able to see beyond the physical world into the archetypal forms that animate it; he is able to establish or reveal a personal link with the archetypal realm. In a sense, such ascetic practices allow spiritual power to irrupt into

the seeker's world. But this is why Black Elk warns against undertaking such practices without a spiritual guide – for without traditional protections one might find malevolent psychic forces intruding themselves into one's psyche, with little means of recognizing whether such forces are malevolent or not until it is too late. For the subtle world includes both beneficent and malevolent forces.

There are communal practices that also lead to visionary experiences. Among these are the Sun Dance of the Plains Indians, in which days of fasting and exhausting dancing and singing – and, years ago, self-inflicted torture – lead to certain kinds of visions. What is more, the symbolism of the dance – the sun, the buffalo and the heart – suggests a kind of communal totemic connection to spiritual truth. One must also mention such practices as ingesting hallucinogenic mushrooms or peyote, common among Mesoamerican or South American tribes. More recently this practice spread to North America through the Native American Church, a pan-Indian movement employing peyote to elicit visions. Naturally, such practices involving hallucinogens must be strictly controlled, since the danger of psychic disequilibrium with the use of drugs is great, but in essence such practices are still linked to vision seeking and to the totemic spiritual guardian traditions.

Our discussion here, while certainly not exhaustive, has illustrated something of how deeply the totemic and guardian spirit traditions are bound up with Native American traditions across the entire length and breadth of the Americas. While there are great differences in terminology, and indeed in practices as well, the fundamental significances of totemic and guardian spirits remain the same. They represent the profound and spiritual interconnection between native peoples, native cultures, and the natural world, all of which derive from the spiritual world and reflect their spiritual origin and meaning. Far from being merely 'fetish worship', totems reveal cosmological and metaphysical significances of which we might do well to take heed.

9

SACRED SITES
IN THE
AMERICAS

From our discussion thus far of Native American traditions, we can see that the American Indian relationship to the natural world is strikingly different from a modern, materialist view of nature. For the traditional tribal man or woman, the natural world is a theatre of religious revelation. As we have seen, birds, animals, plants and stars all can have spiritual significance. Naturally, the same is true of the landscape itself. Thus, across the whole of the Americas, we find native peoples recognizing and augmenting the spiritual significance of the landscape around them, incorporating special sites and places into rituals and spiritual practices. To recognize why and how this is so, is perhaps the most important thing we can learn from a study of Native American traditions.

A sacred site that has been preserved undefiled is the Great Serpent Mound in Ohio, made by the Adena and Hopewell people, who flourished between 100 BC and 700 AD. It is a religious site rather than a burial ground.

THE
ELEMENT
LIBRARY
NATIVE
AMERICAN
TRADITIONS

WESTERN CONSUMERISM
VERSUS THE NATIVE WORLDVIEW

It is remarkable how little Americans have recognized the spiritual significances of sacred places long embraced by Native traditions. Whereas in England, Wales, Ireland and many other European countries, places sacred to indigenous traditions often remained sacred to Christianity too – cathedrals built on holy hills, for instance. The tradition of incorporation also continued in South America and Mesoamerica. In the United States, there is a long history of ignoring and even defiling places sacred to the indigenous peoples. To this day, we have many examples of local, state, and federal governments ignoring Native American pleas and destroying sacred sites. Examples are legion – sacred springs defiled and destroyed, sacred hills mined or otherwise ruined, remote mountaintops logged or rendered useless by new roads. In very few places has Christianity supported the American Indian recognition of sacred places.

The modern American attitude towards the landscape, however – which recognizes in it only something to be 'used up' or 'consumed' – does not derive from Christianity, but from modern industrialism and scientific materialism. The traditional recognition that particular landscapes or sacred places reflect the confluence of spiritual energies, and are places conducive to spiritual revelation, has no place in a worldview that does not recognize the legitimacy of anything other than the accumulation of 'consumer goods' and the merely material value of a given area. A society given to exhaustive mining, gaudy fast food restaurants, and never ending strips of commercialism is about as far from recognizing the spiritual significance of landscape as one can imagine.

In such a society, we certainly have something to learn from indigenous cultures that still recognize the spiritual significance of landscape. For as we have seen, the American Indian cultures live in an integrated world. For them, the stars, the planets, the sun and moon, the hills and rivers, the mountains and the caves, are all part of an integrated cosmological worldview, or cosmovision. What is more, certain places are especially sacred for indigenous peoples; while not everyone in the tribe goes to such places for spiritual practice, the spiritual harmony and welfare of the tribe depends upon some people travelling to those places and maintaining and enriching tribal contact with the spirit realm.

RIGHT Worlds collided when the traditional arts and crafts of Indian cultures met western consumerism. This store is in Nome, Alaska.

OPPOSITE RIGHT Visions of Christian saints often appeared in places that already carried a religious ethos before Christianity took hold. This is Our Lady of Guadeloupe, Mexico.

OPPOSITE FAR RIGHT Jesuit missionaries, backed up by conquistador muscle, persuaded many Native Indians to convert to Catholicism.

EARLY LINKS BETWEEN
CHRISTIANITY AND NATIVE PEOPLES

When European settlers first came to New England, they found on the east coast of America highly developed religious traditions closely integrated to the landscape there. In fact, as James Mavor and Byron Dix have pointed out in their important book Manitou: The Sacred Landscape of New England's Native Civilization (1989), the degree of this cosmological integration with the landscape has certainly not been sufficiently recognized by most historians. All over New England one finds standing stones, stone caves aligned with solstices, or other celestial phenomena. There are stone 'Indian forts', or stone embankments, used for collecting the subtle currents of the landscape, and there are other places which are certainly part of the Native religious traditions.

Mavor and Dix suggest a much longer survival of these traditions of sacred landscape into the modern era than many previous authors have recognized. They argue a much closer connection between some Christian Europeans and Native American tribes than previously recognized. In their studies of many sacred sites in New England, they found evidence that some of these sites are still in use, or at least have been used in modern times. They also found much historical evidence that some tribes, while nominally becoming Christian, retained tribal practices, just as some Christians continued to recognize Indian holy places and incorporated them into Church geography.

Even though, for the most part, Christians in America paid little attention to the Native American traditions regarding sacred landscape, one can find some instances – particularly early on in the history of European contact with Indians – of cultural cross pollination. The history of the Mormons is especially closely linked to American Indian traditions; but all across the Americas, one finds connections between American Indian religion and Christianity. For example, Black

Elk and Fools Crow, among others of the Sioux tribe spiritual leaders, converted to different Christian sects while continuing their native spiritual ways. Then, too, on the far west coast of America, many tribal people became Shaker Christians, retaining many traditional ways. So Christianity and indigenous spirituality are not necessarily inherently opposed.[34]

It is nonetheless the case that, by and large, European or modern Americans have been less than reverential towards Native American ritual sites, to say the least of it. Mavor and Dix write of a particularly remarkable 'rocking stone' formation in Massachusetts, a many-ton boulder standing atop another in the woods – and of how a 'development' company called 'Algonkin' destroyed the site to make it an industrial 'park'. Instances like this can be adduced a thousand times over, from all over the United States. As we have already stated, the most sacred spring in Kansas, Wakonda Spring – to which tribal people from all over the Plains came to make offerings – was defiled and lost under the Glen Elder reservoir. Almost nothing of the once numerous mysterious 'effigy mounds' in the shapes of sacred animals remains in the mid-west, and there are virtually no unvandalized petroglyph sites left.

THE
ELEMENT
LIBRARY
NATIVE
AMERICAN
TRADITIONS

SURVIVING SACRED SITES

There are certainly some sacred sites left in the United States, even if, for the most part, their precise significance is no longer known. All across New England, there are standing stones, 'rocking stones', 'stone forts' – wall enclosures situated near streams or springs on hillsides, as well as sacred stone chambers. Across the mid-west are mound sites, including the Great Serpent Mound in Ohio, as well as many lesser known mounds. In the upper Plains states or high country, are 'medicine wheels', stone circles with astrological alignments; and across the Americas are sacred mountains and other high places on which one is closer to the sky realm, the earth and the horizon spread out below.

These sacred sites can be classified according to their primary elemental character. Sacred enclosures, for example, can be seen as taking advantage of water in that they are often found near the bend of a river or creek, and hence represent the 'accumulation', in their horseshoe shape, of the subtle currents of earth and water. Sacred springs above all represent the power of water. Caves, stone chambers, and sandstone petroglyph bluffs incorporate the power of earth, and the chthonic powers found in the earth. High places and mountains incorporate the symbolism of air and height, in which mounds also participate to a lesser degree.

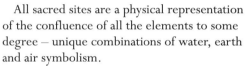
ABOVE *Elephant Rock between Marta and Presipio in Texas, USA.*

BELOW *Sacrificial table at Mystery Hill, Salem, New Hampshire, USA.*

All sacred sites are a physical representation of the confluence of all the elements to some degree – unique combinations of water, earth and air symbolism.

For example, the Lyons Serpent, a 160-foot-long serpent form carved into the earth on a bluff in Kansas, incorporates the symbolism of earth, air and water at once. The Lyons Serpent terraglyph is found at the headwaters of the Little Arkansas River, on the highest bluff in that countryside. Likewise, Mulberry Cave, a sacred cave in Kansas, is above a spring and below a high bluff; the cave itself is directionally oriented, forming a cross pointing east, west, north and south.[35] Indeed, one may say that if every landscape is unique, even more so must every sacred site present unique characteristics.

Virtually all of these sacred sites have one central characteristic in common: celestial alignments. In recent years archaeologists have begun to recognize and study more closely the complex celestial alignments and calculations that mark sacred sites all across the Americas, from Canada to far South America, from New England to the west coast. The precise celestial calculations of southern civilizations like the Maya have long been known – we mentioned earlier the extraordinary astrological calendar. So too, the complex astrological alignments of

buildings, and especially temples in Mesoamerica and South America, have been recognized for many years. However, exactly how much these kinds of alignments also characterized northern tribal sites has not been appreciated or studied for as long, or in as much depth.

Certain alignments are associated with tribal sacred sites across the Americas, and most prevalent are alignments with the winter and summer solstices. Mavor and Dix have shown how many sites in New England are aligned precisely with the solstices, and in some cases with the equinoxes. Likewise, Waldo Wedel and Clark Mallam have shown how the Lyons Serpent is aligned with three 'council mounds' located several miles away, so that the entire alignment connects with celestial phenomena, including the solstices. Demonstrations show that many of the 'medicine wheel' circles found in Canada, Montana and elsewhere in the upper United States, are aligned with solstices and equinoxes.

Medicine Wheels

Many sites reveal complex and obscure alignments. Probably the most well known of the medicine wheels is the Big Horn Medicine Wheel near Sheridan, Wyoming. The Big Horn Medicine Wheel is found in the Big Horn Mountains at an altitude of roughly 9,600 feet, on the shoulder of a mountain. Roughly ninety feet in diameter, the Big Horn wheel consists in a central rock cairn about twelve feet across and two feet high, with twenty-eight radiating spokes made of small stones, encircled by a rim of small stones, with six larger stone piles at strategic points on the rim. It may be that the stone cairns once held wooden posts, which would make of this site a woodhenge, but in any case, the medicine wheel definitely reveals complex celestial alignments.

As John Eddy has reported, the Big Horn Medicine Wheel marks numerous stellar alignments. Eddy found that this medicine wheel, and another he investigated in southern Montana, include primary alignments with the summer solstice dawn and sunset. This is not surprising, since the summer solstice marks the time when the sun's power is at its peak, and corroborates the symbolism of the Sun Dance and other solar rites. But Eddy also found alignments with the rising of the stars Aldebaran, Rigel and Sirius, in the constellations Taurus, Orion and Canis Major respectively. This is particularly interesting, since these stars rise helically (with the sun) twenty-eight days apart, a pattern that began with the rising of Aldebaran at the summer solstice between the years AD 1400 and 1700. There are, as noted earlier, twenty-eight spokes on the Big Horn Medicine Wheel.[36]

The same alignments are found in Moose Mountain Medicine Wheel in Saskatchewan, Canada. Although the Moose Mountain wheel does not have twenty-eight spokes, it too marks the summer solstice dawn and sunset; and it too marks the rising of Aldebaran, Rigel and Sirius with six cairns and a centre cairn. Research suggests that the Moose Mountain wheel may predate the Big Horn Wheel — which it resembles very closely — by more than a thousand years. This, and the distance between the two wheels, leads one to conclude that under consideration here is very ancient shamanic symbolism, directly linking the human, the natural, and the celestial cycles, and incorporating celestial forces largely unrecognized in modern times.[37]

The Big Medicine Wheel at Sedona, Arizona. Medicine Wheels were used for shamanic rituals. Many were marked to align with the positions of major stars.

THE
ELEMENT
LIBRARY
NATIVE
AMERICAN
TRADITIONS

THE SIGNIFICANCE OF
SACRED SITES – A SUMMARY

All these sacred sites in the Americas – from the standing stones of New England to the mounds of the mid-west, to the rock wheels or figures of the high plains or mountains, to the great southern temples of Mesoamerica – retain an enigmatic character for us modern people. We can reconstruct some of the cosmological significance of given sites, but in all too many cases, the traditional meanings and mythological cycles connected to a given astrologically situated sacred site are irretrievably lost. Simply to recognize alignments with Aldebaran, for example, does not tell us what those alignments mean, and of course, what mattered most to the people responsible for these sites is precisely their significance.

At the same time, we can reconstruct something of what certain sacred sites mean, particularly some of the great southern or Mesoamerican temples and cities; for as we noted earlier, the great cities and temples of Mesoamerica were based on the relationship of the human body to the cosmos as a whole. The individual human being, like the traditional culture and the cosmos itself, was centred on the Tree of the cosmos, and had the Sun as its heart. In other words, there is a direct correlation between the individual, or microcosm, the culture, or mesocosm, and the cosmos, or macrocosm. They reflect one another. And their fundamental nature is expressed in architecture, the culture's

Anasazi petroglyphs (stone pictures) made in the 1200s. This is 'Newspaper Rock' in Canyonlands National Park, Utah, USA. A detail is shown below.

manifestation. Certainly exemplary of this relationship is the great city of Teotihuacan, thirty miles north-east of Mexico City. Teotihuacan, as we have noted before, is the most remarkable of the Mesoamerican classic cities, a gigantic feat of cosmovision made manifest in more than seventy-five geomantically situated temples, the entire city laid out in four directionally oriented quadrants marked out by the Avenue of the Dead and the east-west axis. In this enormous terraglyph, the Pyramid of the Sun exemplifies the astrological considerations that informed so much of the city: its stairway of the sun faces directly the place where the Pleiades rises on the horizon on the day when the sun reaches its zenith.

As numerous writers have shown or acknowledged, virtually all of the Mesoamerican and South American temples reveal complex astrological alignments. David Carrasco writes of the Mayan culture:

◎◎

Intimately related to the Maya calendar was the careful alignment of particular buildings and ceremonies with the dramatic cycles and appearances of celestial bodies, including the moon, sun, Venus, and so on … Archaeoastronomy has shown how major temples, entire ceremonial centres, and the calendars that guided ritual and social life were dependent, in part, on astronomical events and patterns.[39]

◎◎

THE PENOKEE MAN

The linking of the human world to natural and celestial cycles can also be seen in a rock formation found in western Kansas, called the Penokee Man. The Penokee Man consists of small rocks laid out in the form of a giant man with upraised arms and large ears. It is found on the highest hillside in that county. There is much evidence of ancient stoneworking in the area. During the nineteenth century, travellers remarked that the whole hillside was marked with stone cairns — since used to build barns and walls and houses — that no doubt also had astrological alignments. Penokee Man is probably aligned with the constellation Orion and with the summer solstice; but its precise astrological significance is as yet unknown.[38] Nonetheless, it remains an enigmatic reminder of how man reflects and is connected to celestial cycles.

for tourists to visit, are not as important as what they mean. A sacred site is sacred because of what it means, because of how it reflects our inherent human connection to the cosmic cycles. Petroglyphs will erode and fall to earth; even great temples will crumble one day. But the meanings of sacred mountains and other places, these do not erode or disappear, for they are borne deep within us as human beings, and confirmed by our traditional inheritance. This, in Native American religions, as in other world religions, is what really matters.

Stone temples rise above the forest canopy at Palenque, Guatemala, relics of the great Mayan city built about AD 624. As well as temples to the many Mayan gods, it contained a palace and a royal tomb.

Given this complex calendar and the profound astrological significances that linked social-religious and natural cycles to celestial cycles, we can see how, in such a world, the buildings themselves became glyphs directly reflecting the order of the universe itself.

This, in fact, is the meaning of sacred sites all across the Americas, not only in Mesoamerica. Sacred sites are special places which manifest the confluence of natural forces, but their power is augmented by being used for rituals by human beings. Teotihuacan was once a sacred cave, and all the efflorescence of rich architectural construction above and around that cave is an elaboration of its fundamental significance, much as the great architectural edifices of Europe, the cathedrals in particular, are architectonic manifestations of the Christian cosmovision. Traditional people, living in such places, are surrounded by the cosmological vision of their tradition, so that the whole world around them reflects spiritual and cosmological truth.

Although it is true that modern American society recognizes virtually nothing of sacred landscape as seen in a traditional culture like that of the Native American, even so America has many sacred sites. But these sites, as places

10

THE
VISIONARY WORLD

Despite the enormous variety of Native American traditions, and of the ways in which these various traditions contact the visionary world, all of them do affirm the existence and power of those realms seen in visions. The more southern traditions, like the Pueblo, emphasize contact with the visionary or archetypal realm through mask rituals, not through individual vision quests like the more northern Plains tribes. But whatever the means of contacting and maintaining contact with the archetypal realm, such contact remains at the centre of all the American Indian tribal traditions. In this discussion, however, we will focus more closely on the Plains Indian narratives of contact with the 'imaginal' visionary world.

The word 'imaginal' was created by the great scholar Henry Corbin to distinguish what he called 'active Imagination' from mere fantasy, or imagination. The active Imagination perceives an actual spiritual reality. Corbin wrote, in his important study Spiritual Body and Celestial Earth, that there is an 'intermediary world, a world of archetypal celestial Figures which the active Imagination alone is able to apprehend. This Imagination does not construct something

Ben Black Elk, a visionary of the modern Sioux nation, integrates traditional ways with modern life.

unreal, but unveils the hidden reality'.[40] It is on this intermediary world shown to us by American Indian visionary narratives that we will concentrate in this chapter.

We will focus primarily on three visionary narratives, all by Sioux holy men: Lame Deer, Fools Crow and Black Elk. The visionary narratives of these three holy men arguably comprise the most influential of all contemporary Indian narratives, and Black Elk in particular has been credited with helping to renew interest in spirituality among many North American Indian tribal peoples. All three of these works exemplify Native American spirituality as expressed in the Sioux tradition. We will focus above all on the narratives of Black Elk, because these most clearly reveal parallels to other world religious traditions. As Joseph Epes Brown has written:

◎◎

If we can understand … the truths the Indians find in their relationships to nature, and the profound values reflected by their many rites and symbols, then we may become enriched, our understanding may deepen, and we shall be able to give to the American Indian heritage its rightful place among the great spiritual traditions of humankind.[41]

◎◎

THE ARCHETYPAL WORLD OF PLATO

The American Indian religious tradition already has its place among the great spiritual and philosophical traditions of mankind. The problem historically has been that modern people have been unable to recognize exactly how this is so, chiefly because the Native American religious traditions are ancient — one might even say primordial — and without scriptures. As a primarily oral tradition without extensive written exposition of metaphysical and cosmological doctrines, the Native American religions have often been regarded as 'primitive' or 'savage'. In order to understand their deeper, visionary significance, it is useful to begin with Plato.

In *The Republic*, Plato offers us the famous allegory of the cave, and suggests that the things of this world are but reflections of their archetypes in the intellectual world. In this dialogue, Socrates says to Glaucon: 'You will not misapprehend me if you interpret the journey upwards to be the ascent of the soul into the intellectual world' (VII.317). When one's soul ascends to the intellectual or archetypal worlds, says Socrates, it does not behold the 'shadows of true existence' and the 'images in the water' of this world, but 'animals and plants and the light of the sun', the 'real animals and stars', and, after the eyes of the spirit have adjusted to accommodate the brightness, 'the sun himself' (VII.532).

Now this concept of ascent to the archetypal realm of which this world is but a reflection is absolutely central to Plato's work, and offers us a way of recognizing in the Graeco-Judaeo-Christian heritage what we will shortly see in the American Indian visionary narratives as well. According to Plato, animals, plants, and other things in this world are physical reflections or manifestations of transcendent archetypes, and the true artist is one who realizes, here below, those archetypes as best he can. The wise man is he who has ascended above the 'cave', who realizes that this world is merely fleeting, and who nonetheless returns to the social world in order to help and to guide his

Socrates (469-399 BC) the great Greek philosopher. In Plato's dialogues, Socrates describes the world outside the 'cave' of mundane existence and how difficult it is to explain to people inside the cave. In just the same way, shamans try to explain their visions of the world beyond the physical.

fellow man to realize the truth and to live a right and proper life.

Plato's work is very much parallel to the Native American tradition here. For in American Indian traditions — and in Sioux tradition in particular — the wise man is also reverenced, for there, as in Plato's *Republic*, he is one whose soul has ascended to the realm of the archetypes, has experienced the spiritual world as it really is, and has then returned to this world and to the world of men, in order to help them. Just as in Plato's work the true artist is enjoined to ascend to the higher realm and then to depict here below archetypal or transcendent reality, so too in American Indian traditions, one finds that the designs on clothing, the archetypal images, the architecture — indeed, all the beautiful and primordial symbolism of the tribes — is created in order to manifest the archetypal or transcendent on earth.

Having written this, we must immediately clarify it. Plato offers us ways of conceptually understanding spiritual experience — but we must emphasize 'conceptual' here. By contrast, the American Indian religious traditions in general are not explained in concepts, but in experiential terms.

THE
ELEMENT
LIBRARY
NATIVE
AMERICAN
TRADITIONS

LAME DEER

Let us take as an example Lame Deer's explanation of how a Sioux holy man, or *wicasa wakan* works. According to Lame Deer, the *wicasa wakan* likes to be alone, away from the crowd and from mundane concerns. He prefers to meditate, leaning against a tree or rock, feeling the earth below him and the weight of the 'big flaming sky' upon him. 'Closing his eyes, he sees many things clearly', Lame Deer tells us. 'What you see with your eyes shut is what counts.' The *wicasa wakan* loves silence, and wraps it around himself like a blanket. He listens to the secret voices of the plants and animals of the earth, Lame Deer tells us, and from all living beings something flows into him and something flows out of him.[42]

Plato and Lame Deer are discussing the same general pattern of the visionary's acting as rapport between the spiritual and the physical – but Lame Deer's version is more an experiential description, hence more mysterious and more visceral.

If we keep in mind this fundamental understanding, then perhaps the universal significance of the three visionary narratives we have chosen to concentrate on will become clearer. Let us consider, for instance, Lame Deer's description of the *wakinyan*, or thunderbirds: he tells us that there are four large, old thunderbirds, foremost among them is the great *wakinyan* of the west, who is clothed in clouds, is formless, and has huge, four-jointed wings. Although the *wakinyan* has no feet, he has enormous claws; and although he has no head, he has large teeth. Lame Deer finds it difficult to describe the *wakinyan*, and turns to paradox, referring to a face without features, a shape without form, claws without feet, eyes that are not eyes.[43] Lame Deer cannot explain in physical terms the nature of the thunderbirds because they are not physical beings; rather, he must use symbolism, explaining by using physical terms in a paradoxical way, to describe that which transcends the physical.

FOOLS CROW

In his narrative, Frank Fools Crow speaks about a healing ceremony with the medicine man, Frank Good Lance. It was a very simple ceremony, without even the three singers most medicine men use, and it was powerful. Fools Crow narrates:

⊛

Frank Good Lance started to sing again, and in the blackness I could feel something flying around inside the room. Then I began to hear bird noises; loud bird noises. I knew immediately what kind of bird it was. It was the chirping of baby eagles. Many times I had found their nests, and heard them make this same sound. Then outside the house and above us I could hear the most wonderful and clear sounds of screaming eagles. It was really something marvellous to experience.[44]

⊛

Here, the archetypal power of the eagles is being called down in a healing ceremony, and so one finds the subtle penetrating into the physical world: they hear the eagles, and see their power manifested in the healing of the man who was supposed to be dying, and who was subsequently healed.

That this is an objectively verifiable reality – that we are not talking here about mere psychological fantasies – is underscored by Frank Fools Crow, he tells us that when someone is engaged in lamenting for a vision under his care, he sees precisely the same vision that they see. Fools Crow says that after the vision-seeker is in his square, he returns to the sweat lodge and stays there 'in deep meditation and prayer, giving them support until they are through'.

He continues:

⊛

Both of us fast while we are there. I share fully in what he is doing, and whatever he sees in his vision, I see too, I see it and when I go to him I can tell him exactly what he saw. The reason some medicine men are not able to do this is that after they have placed their pledges they get into their automobiles and go shopping or get a bottle and have a party … I don't do this. The vision quest is too sacred, too holy. I want to share completely with them and give them my full support. I want us to be of one mind, and I want to feel and suffer with them.[45]

⊛

BLACK ELK

In Black Elk's visionary narrative, we see all the elements we have discussed joined together. One might say that Black Elk's great vision, granted him when he was nine-years-old, represents an extremely intense manifestation of the same kinds of experiences common among the three narratives. Lame Deer, Fools Crow, and Black Elk each spoke with animals, birds, or stones; but in Black Elk's great vision it is as if this power of revelation through beings in animal form is intensified almost beyond bearing. Black Elk talked about how he had fallen ill, and laid as if dead in a tipi for twelve days, during which time he was in 'a wonderful place'.[46]

In this, Black Elk's first and most powerful vision, he was greeted and escorted by horses, celestial horses of the four directions, and saw the celestial archetypes of all beings. There were twelve horses in each of the four directions, and their colours corresponded to the directional colours; there was, he said, a 'skyful of horses dancing all around me'.[47] The horses changed into all the countless 'animals of every kind, and all the fowls that are', and disappeared back into the four directions.[48] Then he saw the Six Grandfathers, and each of them spoke to him; after which he saw the suffering his people were to endure. A black stallion then sang him a song, and its song went out over all the universe, and was marvellous to hear. In Black Elk's words:

There was nothing that did not hear, and ... it was so beautiful that nothing anywhere could keep from dancing. The virgins danced, and all the circled horses. The leaves on the trees, the grasses on the hills and in the valleys, the waters in the creeks and in the rivers and the lakes, the four-legged and the two-legged and the wings of the air — all danced together to the music of the stallion's song.[49]

Knowledge gained in dreams and visions was considered as important and relevant as anything learned in waking life. Sacred Otter, a Blackfoot buffalo hunter, dreamed a vision of the tipi of Es-Tonea-Pesta, the Lord of Cold Weather. The symbols on the tipi told Sacred Ottter how to help and protect his people.

Black Elk was given a paradisal vision:

The whole wide circle of the day was beautiful and green, with all fruits growing and all things kind and happy.[50]

These are indeed paradisal images; and Black Elk tells us that he was at the sacred mountain at the centre of the world, at the *'place where the sun continually shines'*.[51]
He continues:

... while I stood there I saw more than I can tell and I understood more than I saw, for I was seeing in a sacred manner the shapes of all things in the spirit, and the shape of all shapes as they must live together in one being.[52]

After his vision was over, it remained in him *'like a strange power glowing in my body; but when the part of me that talks would try to make words for the meaning, it would be like fog and get away from me'.[53]*

Black Elk emphasizes the transcendent power of his vision, beyond what words can say:

It was the pictures I remembered and the words that went with them; for nothing I have ever seen with my eyes was so clear and bright as what my vision showed me; and no words that I have ever heard with my ears were like the words I heard. I did not have to remember these things; they have remembered themselves all these years. It was as I grew older that the meanings came clearer and clearer out of the pictures and the words; and even now I know that more was shown to me than I can tell.[54]

THE
ELEMENT
LIBRARY
NATIVE
AMERICAN
TRADITIONS

Totems and visions offered powerful protection. A young Indian, sent to seek Utonagan, the female guardian spirit of his ancestors, is protected by his tribe's totem, the wolf, as he sleeps.

He did not have to remember these images and words, for they remembered themselves. Statements like these make more sense to us when we recall Plato's allegory of the cave, and what it is like for the man who returns to the physical world after having seen the archetypal realm of unceasing light. He tries to tell the others in the cave what the transcendent realm is like, but it is very difficult, for although one speaks in words that seem to convey reality, they cannot really do so. Modern man, conditioned by the contemporary emphasis upon historicism and on the physical world as alone possessing validity, finds it hard to understand visionary narratives precisely because their fundamental premise is that the physical world is subordinate to the transcendent realms. It is difficult for us to conceive that the human being may be able to enter, through vision, into the realms into which he is destined to pass after death. American Indian visionary narratives take a special place among world religions precisely because they remind us so

clearly of the relation between this earth and the spiritual realities it bodies forth before us.

As the Swedish scholar of Native American traditions, Ake Hultkranz, has written, the time is not long past when tribal peoples were regarded by whites as having no religion whatever, or even as worshipping the devil. Given this prejudice – which is by no means completely vanquished yet from American society – Native American visionary narratives take on a special importance in revealing the religious centre of the traditions they embody, and in showing us how the Native American religious traditions must be accorded their place among the world religions.[55] If they are to survive, these traditions must be recognized by modern society as worthy of respect, and visionary narratives play an essential role, not only in providing a way towards this recognition, but in reminding us of the imaginal realm to which we are all heir, and through which, according to these religious traditions, we are destined to pass if we live a worthy life.

11

SACRED ART
AND MYTHOLOGY

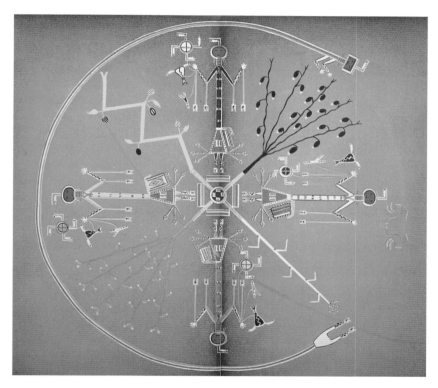

Native American traditions present a rich, and sometimes bewildering variety of sacred art. From Navajo chantways to Hopi *kachinas*, from sacred clothing designs to sacred masks, all across the Americas the indigenous peoples have produced works of art indivisible from the religious and cosmological visions that they body forth. And this is in fact the key to the extraordinary range of Native American art: however disparate its manifestations, they are always directly linked to a mythological cycle, and hence reflect spiritual and cosmological truth. In short, traditional art among the Native American peoples is always sacred; and it is sacred because it bears a message of the transcendent.

Here again we have a fundamental difference from the modern view, this time of art. Traditional art, particularly in Native American cultures, is indivisibly linked to its religious symbolism. Philip Sherrard writes:

☙

A spiritual or sacred art ... presupposes a way of life centred in the knowledge and experience — or, rather, in a knowledge that is the experience — of spiritual realities. It presupposes a metaphysical view of the universe, one that sees reality as issuing from God in successive levels — levels that may be summarized as the spiritual, the psychic, and the physical.[56]

☙

Navajo sand painting from the Yeibachai or Night Way Chart showing the sixteen Black fire Gods.
➤

THE
ELEMENT
LIBRARY
NATIVE
AMERICAN
TRADITIONS

LEFT *Kachina dolls were made by the Hopi Indians for their children to play with so that they would learn to recognize the Kachina (spirit being) masks worn by religious leaders and understand the significance of each Kachina.*

Much modern art, conversely, excludes an authentic religious centre, and is limited to physical and psychological dimensions. Because most modern art — abstract or realist, surreal or otherwise — lacks a spiritual dimension, many modern people erroneously ignore that dimension in traditional art as well. This is a mistake.

For in a traditional culture, and certainly in Native American cultures, everything in the culture bears the stamp of its spiritual centre. Indeed, this is true not only of cultural artifacts like temple orientation, construction and decoration, but even of the natural world itself, for trees, waters, mountains, animals, winds, all remind the people of particular mythological cycles that in turn bear spiritual messages. One's clothing, including its designs, the building in which one lives, the lodges one constructs for purification or initiation ceremonies, the tools one carries, all these things bear sacred designs that remind people of their spiritual purpose and their meaning.

Thomas Yellowtail, Crow medicine man and Sun Dance chief, emphasizes this point:

BELOW *Navajo sand paintings were more than just pictures. Some paintings were part of a healing ritual, with the sand painting representing the creation of the world and encouraging a rebalancing of the sick person's psyche within the world.*

It is important that the young people understand the difference between the traditional ways and the modern world we live in today. I have spoken before about the sacred support that was always present for the traditional Indians. With this support, from the moment you arose and said your first prayer until the moment you went to sleep you could at least see what was necessary in order to lead a proper life. Even the dress that you wore every day had sacred meanings, such as the bead work designs on the clothing, and wherever you went or whatever you did, whether you were hunting, making weapons, or whatever you were doing, you were participating in a sacred life and you knew who you were and carried a sense of the sacred with you. All of the forms had meaning, even the tipi and the sacred circle of the entire camp. Of course the life was hard and difficult, and not all Indians followed the rules. But the support of the traditional life and the presence of Nature everywhere brought great blessings on all the people.[57]

The point Yellowtail makes here is critical, and cannot be emphasized enough.

Some modern commentators on American Indian art or architecture assert that traditional artifacts or buildings or ritual sacred sites were made, like modern abstract art, merely for 'aesthetic' pleasure. But in fact, traditional art in Native American cultures has one central purpose: to remind us of our spiritual purpose in life, to help us live in the right way, and to prepare us for the afterlife. It is mistaken to view traditional art through secular modern eyes; one can do so, but only by ignoring sacred meanings. All traditional art is designed to remind its viewers and users of how they and their world reflect spiritual realities — for traditional art is not on display as an exhibit in a traditional society, but is used daily.

SACRED ART ON OBJECTS OF DAILY USE

Let us then turn to some specific forms of traditional Native American art. Plains Indian clothing reflects spiritual symbolism, and this 'vestimentary art' also extends by analogy to other tribes. For instance, the eagle feather represents the Great Spirit, and the rosette of eagle feathers or of porcupine quills represents the sun. To wear the eagle feather head-dress is to be identified with the sun as spiritual centre, and this is to confer on the wearer a spiritual dignity partaking of royalty; not just anyone wears such a head-dress.

Certain designs, made out of quill-work or beadwork – the latter introduced by European trade and allowing precise geometric symbolism on garments or other objects – also reflect cosmological symbolism. Some designs show the four directions, others thunder beings, other certain clan or tribal patterns. Such designs may be found on garments, on blankets, on pouches, on moccasins, and tipis, among many other objects. Fringes suggest the symbolism of rain. But in all cases, these designs have meanings, and reflect back to the user the spiritual and cosmological significance of that object. Thus one's clothes, dwelling, and objects of daily use are marked through designs to remind users of their spiritual purpose and meaning.

BELOW *Richly beaded garments, and hair braids symbolize the wealth of this girl's Eskimo family. She is of marriageable age and dressed to attract an acceptable suitor.*

ABOVE *The beautifully crafted feathered war bonnet worn by a tribal chief carried spiritual power as well as signifying his status.*

BELOW *Colourful baskets woven by the Moki Indians used patterns to depict natural forces such as the flow of water.*

THE
ELEMENT
LIBRARY
NATIVE
AMERICAN
TRADITIONS

SACRED ART IN
DANCE COSTUMES AND MASKS

If this purpose is true of clothing and daily implements, it is even more true of the ceremonial art of dances.

ABOVE *The Navajo originally learned how to weave from Pueblo Indians. The nomadic Navajo often raided the settled Pueblo villages for food and goods, but eventually learned many skills from them including sheep-raising and fruit growing.*

The Summer Solstice Dance

We have already discussed the symbolism of the Hopi kachinas, the spirit-beings who appear not only in small figurine forms, but in masks and dances as well.

It may be useful, however, to describe the *Niman Kachina*, or summer solstice dance, and in particular some of the dancers. There are eight *hemis kachinas*, or 'far-away kachinas', whose bodies are painted black with white symbols on their chests and backs. Spruce branches hang from their belts; in their right hand each carries a rattle; in the left hand each carries a spruce twig and a downy feather. Deer-hoof and turtleshell rattles clatter on the right leg, bells ring on the left. On the neck is a ruff of spruce, and the face is painted yellow on the left side, blue on the right, while above is a tiara of wild wheat and downy eagle feathers. Above the face is a red rainbow on a white field; above the head are parrot and eagle feathers.[58]

Now all of this colourful symbolism is rooted in the nature of the *kachinas* whom it represents. The dance itself – like so many ritual events across tribal America – takes place near the summer solstice, and as we can see from the many natural objects incorporated into the dance costumes, is bound up with the symbolism of the natural world. The dancer in fact embodies the union of cultural, celestial and natural cycles and forces; he becomes the embodiment, for a time, of the *kachina* itself, and in this sense realizes a state more than human, not only for his own benefit, but for that of the tribe as a whole, and even for the whole world and cosmos.

ABOVE *A young bride of the Wisham Indians dressed in traditional wedding clothes. Most marriages were arranged.*

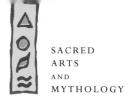

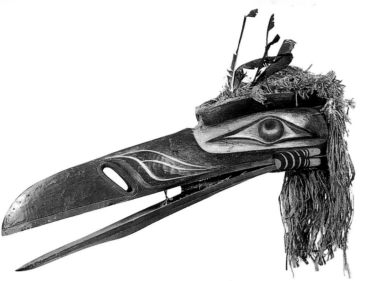

A Crooked-Beak mask used in ceremonies practised by the Indians of the north-west coast.

Zuni Mask Dances

Among the Zuni, another Pueblo tribe of the American south-west, there are also *kachinas* and mask dances. In fact, the Zuni have more than one hundred masks, all very carefully crafted and each representing a particular spirit-being. The most ancient of these masks have special guardians and are kept hidden away, and require special precautions or preparations, including sexual continence, before being worn. Masks include complex sacred geometric diagrams or forms, special natural symbolism like downy feathers or deer antlers, and are often exaggerated in features.[59] As always, sacred art here is a matter of symbolism and function.

The function of these masks is seen primarily in the sacred dances, which among the Zuni, as among the Hopi, are organized around the winter and summer solstices. Like the Hopi festivals, Zuni festivals entail the real presence of the spirit-beings represented in the masks; and like Native American rituals in general, their purpose is to augment and renew the spiritual and subtle forces that in turn animate the physical world and its natural cycles. Summer dances in particular are centred around the growing of maize, which is at once a crop and possessed of profound spiritual symbolism. Maize is at the centre of a way of life, and manifested in the 'medicine objects' or 'fetishes' as well as in masks, sand paintings and other forms of sacred art.

The Pawnee Deer Dance

Other tribal dances may be less colourful, but nonetheless incorporate similar principles. Pawnee participants in the Deer Dance would not be quite as brightly attired as the Hopi or

Zuni dancers, but still certainly embody in that dance an equally complex cosmological symbolism. Here, as in the Hopi ceremony, one's place in the ritual is directionally determined and is part of a whole constellation of symbols and traditions. The Pawnee ceremony takes place in a circular ten-post earth lodge that represents the cosmos, with a fire in the centre, and arrayed around the lodge are groups of the younger, older and elder participants.[60]

The Iroquois False Face Society

As one travels north through the Americas, the dance costumes and symbolism grow somewhat less colourful than those of southern traditions, but the symbolism involved is no less complex, and no less related to the celestial cycles and to natural creatures. There are definitely exceptions to this tendency, as for example the Iroquois 'false face' society on the eastern side of America, not to mention the traditions of the Kwakiutl and other tribes on the northern west coast of North America. In these traditions, too, dances take place at special times of the year and, as in more southern traditions, dancers embody spirit-beings marked by natural symbolism.

The Iroquois 'false face' society was essentially a medicine society in which members would put on grotesque and elaborate masks, thus taking on the characteristics of the beings they represented, and they would then be able to cure people in the tribe who were ailing or afflicted. Wearing these masks and carrying turtle-shell rattles, the false face members accepted tobacco offerings and moved about among the people at certain times of the year curing them. Like the southern dances of the Hopi and other tribes, the Iroquois festivals were part of an agrarian calendar and emphasized the assumption and continuation of traditional powers, rather than individual shamanic experience of the far northern tribes. Masks and rattles, therefore, are means of this assumption and continuation.

THE
ELEMENT
LIBRARY
NATIVE
AMERICAN
TRADITIONS

THE ROLE OF THE MYTH

In essence, such traditional mask festivals are means by which the mythological traditions, and the timeless, archetypal realm they reveal, can be 'grounded' among tribal members in the present. The great scholar A. K. Coomaraswamy once wrote that 'Myth is to history as Universal is to particula'.[61] By this he meant to point out in a different way what we have been saying all along about the relationship of the archetypal to the phenomenal world. Myth speaks in an intimate way to the soul of the archetypal realm informing the physical world. It reminds us, through the artistic means of mask, dance, song, poem, story and other ritual accoutrements, of the archetypal world, through what Joseph Epes Brown calls 'the immediacy of the mythological message'.

While abstract religious teachings are both necessary and powerful – as one sees in such works as the *Tao te ching* and the Upanishads – they are by no means the only way of conveying spiritual truth to people, nor of allowing people to participate directly in spiritual reality. It is no coincidence that medieval Christian Europe held great pageants at certain times of the year, sponsored by guilds – for in this way, people participated directly in the archetypal truths represented in the mysteries of the mythological beings in the pageants. Far from a mere popular accretion, such pageants were, like American Indian mythological recitals and festivals, ways to directly participate in religious mysteries.

Thus, myths and the religious festivals linked to them are certainly not just 'fiction', or 'entertainment', although they are entertaining. Rather, they not only remind the soul of the timeless, archetypal realm, they allow it to participate in that realm. Myths reveal the connections between human beings and the natural world by reminding us of the spiritual origin of all things, both human and natural. Hence, mythology links together the world around us; it reveals both our own and nature's significance and explains through parables, symbols and spiritual beings.

The Pawnee Myth of the Wolf Star

An example of how myths accomplish these things can be seen in the Pawnee myth for the origin of the Skidi or Wolf clan. According to this myth, Paruksti, or the wonderful power affiliated with thunderstorms, came out of the west to inspect creation. Now before creation, the gods forgot to invite the Wolf Star, Sirius, to the Council, and so he resented them, and especially Paruksti. Thus the Wolf Star sent a wolf on earth to follow Paruksti. Paruksti carried the people in a whirlwind bag, which he would set down on earth and open when he was tired or lonely. There the people would come out, set up camp, and hunt buffalo. One day, while Paruksti was asleep with his head on the whirlwind bag, the wolf crept up and stole off with the bag. The people came out and found themselves in a barren place without game, so they entertained the wolf at a feast of dried meat. When they discovered who he was, though, they killed him, and this greatly displeased Paruksti, who said that by doing this the people had introduced death among themselves. They would thereafter be known as the Wolf clan, or Skidi Pawnee, and would carry a sacred bundle made of wolf skin.[62]

This Pawnee myth exemplifies the intersection of historical and mythical time that characterizes mythology generally. Mircea Eliade, the great historian of religions, wrote in his classic *Patterns in Comparative Religion*, that even though mythical time is 'transhistoric' or eternal, it has 'in history, a beginning – namely, that moment when the divinity created the world or set it in order, or that moment when the ancestor of civilizing hero made the revelation of any given activity'.[63] In this Pawnee myth of Paruksti and the Wolf Star, we see precisely the beginning of historical time for the Skidi band of Pawnee; we see the introduction of death itself, and the nature of sacrifice that the wolf bundle paradoxically embodies for the tribe.[64]

In other words, in this myth of Paruksti and the Wolf Star, we see commemorated the emergence of time itself through the penetration of archetypal beings into the temporal realm; we see what amounts to a 'fall of man' into time and death, but see also a return to primordial or mythical time. This fall of man in a certain sense 'predates' creation and history, inasmuch as the Wolf Star was left out of the celestial council. But the consequences of the fall, including death for people, come precisely at the intersection of mythical time and human or historical time. However, we must remember that the way down is also the way up; if people erred in killing the wolf, they were also given the sacrificial bundle to remind them of the archetypal, or eternal time in which they existed when creation was new. Therefore, in ritual remembrance, in ritual expression of the myth, tribespeople not only reiterate the fall of man, but return to mythical or archetypal time through the rites.

This is the centre of mythology, and of the ritual and cultural traditions that remind us of it: the myth reminds us of transcendent or archetypal timelessness, in a sense, returns us to it. What matters in the mythological tradition is not history in any modern sense, but what takes place in the Great Time, or mythical time, irrupting into the temporal realm. Modern views of history are, for the Native American, devoid of meaning because they are not informed by a mythological or archetypal, timeless origin. American Indian tribal cultures, their works of art and artifacts and buildings, are all filled with meaning because they reflect exactly this transcendent, archetypal realm of the myths.

We cannot here consider in detail the astonishing diversity of Native American myths, which range from those of the Eskimo of the far north, to those of the Maya and Aztecs and tribes of the far south. But we can recognize the fundamental perspective common to all these different tribal mythologies and traditions; and that is what our approach has sought to accomplish. Above all, we must recognize the nature of archetypal or mythical time, and how to practise certain rituals to encounter that mythical time anew, to contact it and to place the world closer in harmony with it.

12

CIRCLE AND CROSS

Cycles in Native American Traditions

When European culture clashed with Native American
traditions, the Native Americans were the losers.
Their lives were disrupted and fragmented, as were their
sacred rituals. In 1838, the entire Cherokee nation
were displaced from their eastern woodlands home
to the reservations on the Great Plains.

LINEAR TIME VERSUS CYCLIC TIME

Throughout our discussion of Native American traditions, we have drawn attention to the fundamental differences between the traditional American Indian understanding of the cosmos, and modern views. As we have seen, such differences derive from this essential distinction: while the American Indian understanding of the cosmos is a religious one, the modern perspective is secular, materialist, and even anti-religious. From this essential difference in understanding derive the radically divergent views of time we see in Native American traditions and in modernity. At heart, the modern world is based in evolutionary, linear, historicist time; while that of the traditional American Indian is based in cyclical, sacred time.

When modern European people overran the North American continent during the mid and late nineteenth century, they were acting, by and large, on a worldview that had been radically desacralized. Although Christianity, of course, still existed, it had to a considerable extent been overtaken by a materialistic, scientistic worldview that became extremely

powerful during the second half of the nineteenth century, with the advent of Darwinist, evolutionist views of 'progress'. Indeed, much of American 'mainstream' Protestantism was – and still largely is – concerned with how to 'integrate' Christianity with this secularized, materialistic, evolutionist view of time.

This modern view of time as linear and representing 'progress' had definite consequences for American Indian peoples, whose world was still completely informed by a traditional temporal cyclicity. Modern belief in the 'myth of progress' allowed modern society to hold itself and its representatives as 'advanced' or 'developed' peoples, whereas tribal peoples could be labelled 'primitive', 'backward', or, least disparagingly, as 'developing' (presumably into modern 'consumers'). The modern belief in 'progress' in turn led to governmentally sanctioned programmes in America to obliterate Native American cultures and religious traditions and languages, ranging from making traditional rituals illegal – including 'giveaways' (where someone gives

THE
ELEMENT
LIBRARY
NATIVE
AMERICAN
TRADITIONS

away many of his belongings as gifts) – to forced sterilization.

This side of American history must be faced, and its roots in a non-traditional view of time recognized. For European/American destruction of Native American traditions was directly rooted in and justified by this notion of 'progress', which in turn derived from the decidedly anti-traditional theory of evolution. Because most modern European people in America (although there certainly were Christian opponents of materialism)[65] lived in a world from which traditional, sacred, cyclic time had been largely eliminated, it is not surprising that American society would not only fail to recognize, but even actively oppose, that traditional worldview where it still existed among native peoples.

But no tradition in the world, including medieval European Christianity, affirms the idea of historical, linear 'progress'. Rather, for Hindus and Buddhists, for Christians, Jews and Muslims, for the ancient Greeks and for the northern European tribal peoples, as for indigenous American tribal peoples, time is seen to move through cycles, from a Golden and a Silver, to a Bronze and an Iron Age, in which we now live. If the Golden Age is serene and harmonious, the Iron Age in which we now find ourselves is one of cultural fragmentation and ecological destruction. The Sioux myth – according to which in ancient times the sacred buffalo stood on four legs,

Big Foot, the Sioux leader, murdered by US soldiers at the massacre of Wounded Knee in December 1890, along with 350 of his people. His death symbolized the temporary death of the Sioux nation.

and now, in our own time, is rather unsteadily standing on one leg – corresponds exactly to the Hindu myth of the four Ages and its own association of our Iron Age with a now one-legged cow.[66] This is, no doubt, the precise opposite of 'progress'.

In a rather politically charged document called *A Basic Call to Consciousness: The Hau de no sau nee Address to the Western World* (1978), the Six Nations of the Iroquois described European and American history from an American Indian perspective. Needless to say, the view they offer does not embrace the modern concept of 'progress'. The *Hau de no sau nee* write:

∞

Today the species of Man is facing a question of the very survival of the species. The way of life known as Western Civilization is on a death path on which their own culture has no viable answers. When faced with the reality of their own destructiveness, they can only go forward into areas of more efficient destruction …

∞

The air is foul, the waters poisoned, the trees dying, the animals disappearing. We think even the systems of weather are changing. Our ancient teachings warned us that if Man interfered with the Natural laws, these things would come to be. When the last of the Natural Way of Life is gone, all hope for human survival will be gone with it …

∞

But our essential message to the world is a basic call to consciousness. The destruction of the Native cultures and people is the same process which has destroyed and is destroying life on this planet … That process is Western Civilization … [I]f there is to be a future for all beings on this planet, we must begin to seek the avenues of change.[67]

∞

This *Hau de no sau nee* critique of modern civilization is harsh, yet it is a critique also voiced independently not only by many other traditional Native leaders, but also by a growing number of people from modern society itself.

THE CROSS WITHIN THE CIRCLE

More and more people today are becoming aware of the multiple crises we face, not only in the ecological sphere, but in the social sphere as well, indeed, there are so many crises that it seems our world is falling apart. However, relatively few people consider the reasons for this fragmentation. We look for solutions to these crises in science and materialism itself, without recognizing that the scientist, materialistic perspective, which derives from a desacralized, linear worldview, is itself responsible for the crises we face. Hence the Iroquois, like other native peoples and traditional religious leaders or elders around the world, point us not towards scientistic solutions to modern problems, but towards a change in consciousness.

This consciousness can be best represented in the traditional American Indian symbol of the cross within the circle. How does the cross within the circle signify traditional Native American consciousness? In a very real

LEFT *Variants on the circle and cross symbol were used. Here a Shoshone chief draws the symbol in the sand to instruct his pupils.*

sense, this symbol connects and incorporates all that we have said earlier about differences between the modern and the traditional American Indian ways of viewing the world. For the circle signifies the cyclical nature of traditional cosmology, and the cross marks its four points, also the four seasons, and the four ages of traditional time cycles. Standing in the centre of the earth's circle, beneath the sky's circle, in a traditional American Indian culture

BELOW *The power of the circle was central to many Native American rituals. This is a fertility rite performed by Indians from Virginia in 1590.*

THE
ELEMENT
LIBRARY
NATIVE
AMERICAN
TRADITIONS

one is also standing in a world that is permeated by the spiritual.

This integrated consciousness, symbolized by the cross in the circle, is profoundly different from the secular, materialistic consciousness of modern scientism, for instance. In traditional, integrated consciousness, man, his culture, and the four points of his world all reflect their spiritual origin. Far from being merely the result of a mechanistic series of linear events governed by randomness or even by 'chaos', as some would have it these days, the traditional Native American cosmos is completely informed by its spiritual origin, function, and purpose. The four directions are informed by the 'vertical' dimension of sacredness.

Indeed, as Rene Guenon, among other writers, has pointed out, the symbol of the cross is by no means only Christian but in fact bears forth a common symbolism in many traditions, including Hinduism, on which he drew for his classic study *The Symbolism of the Cross* (trs. 1958). As Guenon observes, the vertical axis of the cross represents the world axis or the 'tree at the centre of the worlds', and the celestial ray of manifestation at the centre of all states of being. This means that the vertical axis of the cross, or world-tree or Pole, represents the connection between heaven and earth – precisely the symbolism found in Native American traditions, both northern and southern.

Hence, while the horizontal bar of the cross represents time, or history (within the horizontal circle of nature), the vertical axis is the irruption of timelessness into time, the hierophany of myth, the irradiating centre of the human being and of the cosmos as a whole. This is why in the Plains Indian Sun Dance, for example, the Sun Dance lodge is built around the symbolism of the Centre Pole, a tree crowned by a buffalo head and aligned with the eastern sun. This Centre Pole is surrounded by a circle of twelve smaller poles, which Sun Dance chief Thomas Yellowtail explains as representing the circle of a twelve-moon year, and the circle of earth, which is round.[68] The Centre Pole is the world axis; the circle of lodge poles is the

horizontal level of the cross, and nature's circles or cycles.

This symbolism is found again and again in Native American traditional rituals and architecture. We have seen how the great cities of Mesoamerica were organized around the four directional quarters, so that the cities themselves embodied the glyph of the circle and the cross. So too, the Pawnee sacred lodges incorporated the symbolism of the Centre Pole and the directional cross within a circle, with all the affiliated directional symbolism. Likewise, Sioux sacred rituals incorporate the symbolism of the vertical axis, the cross of four directions, and the horizon's circle – as do Winnebago, Hopi, and many other traditions. This fundamentally allied symbolism is not so much a result of 'cultural diffusion' across the Americas, as a reflection of a primordial and archetypal symbolic truth.

Thus, the meaning of this symbolism for living life is important. According to the famous Black Elk, in the Sioux tradition the east–west road is the path of 'one of who is distracted, who is ruled by his senses, and who lives for himself rather than for his people'. By contrast, the 'red road' of the south–north axis is the good road, corresponding to the 'straight and narrow path' of Christianity, and to the vertical axis of the cross, since to go north is also to go toward the Pole, the cosmic axis.[69] Although the axial symbolism here is transposed to the south–north direction, its significance remains: an integrated and good human life is one oriented toward its sacred meaning, represented in the Pole.

As we have seen, from a Native American perspective, the modern worldview lacks depth or dimension. Restricted largely to the materialistic, scientific, or historical viewpoint, the modern worldview excludes the concepts of sacred sites, of a three-fold hierarchy of being, of a religious cultural centre, of nature's sacredness, and of how we human beings are called to realize on this earth, as best we can, the vertical axis of being that alone confers on life its transcendent meaning. These ideas are absolutely fundamental to the Native American traditions.

PROPHECIES OF THE END TIMES

The problems we face in the modern world – derived from this modern denial or ignorance of sacred truth – are explained within Native American traditions. Many American Indian traditions, from the Mayan to the Hopi, to the Sioux to the Crow (to name but a few), speak of prophecies. The Sioux, Fools Crow, said outright that we are now in the end times of our present time cycle, and that the two witnesses spoken of in the Christian Bible, in Revelation, are now walking upon the earth as predicted in Sioux tradition too. Likewise, Thomas Yellowtail tells us that the Crow tradition prophesies that when a certain sacred plant can no longer be gathered, that will be the end of the present time cycle. Currently, from year to year, it is questionable whether the plant will be gathered.[70] Hopi elders, like Thomas Banyacya, also speak of their tradition's prophecies for our era as an 'end time'.

Essentially, all of these Native American prophecies hold that our present time cycle will come to an end when the sacred ways have been overcome or exhausted, and mankind lives in a completely secularized, fragmented world, overcome by strife,

suffering, egotism, and hatred. The Hopi express this by saying that the end time will be marked by a *kachina* removing his mask and exposing himself before the uninitiated children in the plaza. This will mark the end of Hopi ceremonialism for a while, until the new era begins. For even though this present time cycle will come to an end, another will begin, an emergence into a 'fifth world' according to the Hopi, into a renewed, reconsecrated sacred age.

In this cyclicity, we can see how even though the Native American traditions, like the other great world religions, do not accept the modern notion of 'progress', this does not mean that these traditions are pessimistic. For they maintain their traditional recognition that time is not linear, but cyclical, and that even though we are in the old age of our present era, what was true in antiquity is true today, that man's proper place and function in this world remains ever the same, as symbolized by the axial centre of the circled cross. There is a profound wisdom in this serene and cyclical view of life, one may even say an optimism, and certainly an affirmation of perennial truth.

ABOVE *Tecumseh (1765?-1813), the chief of the Shawnee, tried in vain to unite all American Indians to defend their land against the plundering whites. He travelled around the country rallying support between 1809 and 1813, when he was killed fighting on the British side in the War of 1813. After his death, the Indians living in the mid-west lost hope and resistance crumbled.*

LEFT *It was the Iron Horse that finally defeated the Indians. The railroad made it easier for settlers to move across the country and for large, defensible towns to be built.*

CONCLUSION

*A resurgent interest in spiritual traditions of Native Americans
and an urge to reconcile differences led Pope John Paul II,
head of the Roman Catholic church, to meet Emmett White,
a medicine man of the Pima nation in 1987.*

CONCLUSION

It is certainly true that the Native American traditions, like all the world religions, have been somewhat eroded by the events of the past several hundred years. Some people have gone so far as to suggest that the American Indian religious traditions, practically speaking, have been virtually obliterated by the onslaughts of modernity, and it is no doubt true that many aspects of indigenous religious ritual and culture have indeed been lost forever. From one end of the Americas to the other, all the various tribal traditions have lost cultural unity and rituals. Yet at the same time, these many Native American traditions all affirm primordial and essential values, and because of this have not only an exceptional resilience, but something extraordinarily important to say to the modern world as well.

The past several hundred years have seen the obliteration of entire tribes and cultures. The Aztec empire, for example, disappeared soon after European contact, and so sudden was its passing that one has to wonder if this was not the ordained fall of a culture at the end of its cycle. On the other hand, entire tribes died out during the nineteenth century as a result of infection with European diseases. British painter George Catlin captured in words and in paintings the way of life of the Mandan tribe, and only a few years later, the tribe he visited had died out. The list of tribes and rituals lost over recent centuries is sadly long indeed.

Thomas Yellowtail tells us that some traditional powers and rituals have been withdrawn from native peoples because they are no longer able to practise them properly. He says:

⊚⊚

Back in the days when we were free, when our people knew more about Nature and important things, almost every man had medicine powers, and the only life people knew was centred on the sacred. The real medicine man could do wonders in those days. It is really the modern world and 'civilization' that is causing us to lose all these things. In olden times, the people had their values centred on spiritual concerns. The spiritual powers, the givers of medicines, are taking those sacred things back from us because we do not know how to care for them correctly.[71]

⊚⊚

In other words, if the modern world is responsible for eroding sacred traditions, so too are the people who succumb to modern temptations, and who allow the sacred ways to be lost.

Probably the saddest of all commentaries on this situation is to be found in the words of Black Elk in the famous book Black Elk Speaks. Speaking of the time just after the terrible battle at Wounded Knee in 1890, when the Sioux decided to surrender to the whites, Black Elk said:

⊚⊚

And so it was all over.
I did not know then how much was ended. When I look back now from this high hill of my old age, I can still see the butchered women and children lying heaped and scattered all along the crooked gulch as plain as when I saw them with eyes still young. And I can see that something else died there in the bloody mud and was buried in the blizzard. A people's dream died there. It was a beautiful dream.

⊚⊚

And I, to whom so great a vision was given in my youth — you see me now a pitiful old man who has done nothing, for the nation's hope is broken and scattered. There is no centre any longer, and the sacred tree is dead.[72]

⊚⊚

Black Elk's account remains the most moving ever of this fateful time for the peoples of the Plains.[73]

It was anger over events such as those at Wounded Knee in 1890, and the many injustices done to the Indian peoples across America since, that led to the politically active group AIM (the American Indian Movement) from the 1970s onward. Originally, AIM was allied to tribal spiritual traditions, but the movement became more radical and took up arms, a situation culminating in the well-known stand-off in 1973 between the United States government, particularly the FBI, and the tribal people in AIM. Although there are some American Indian people who support politically radical groups, traditional spiritual leaders have not supported such action, saying that Indians should not take up arms in this

87

THE
ELEMENT
LIBRARY
NATIVE
AMERICAN
TRADITIONS

way, but should follow their traditional spiritual ways instead.

Throughout our discussion of American Indian traditions, we have emphasized the differences between the modern view of the world and the traditions of tribal people and of religious people generally. This conflict cannot be overlooked, for it is at the very heart of the tragedy of the Native American peoples. In the history of the Americas, we see peoples who affirm primordial traditional values based in the premises discussed in this book – the noble warrior ethos, a recognition of nature's spiritual meanings, a profound multidimensional cosmology, a recognition of the relationship between this life and the afterlife – in direct conflict with many modern people who steadfastly deny the existence of all these premises.

The results of this denial have been documented enough elsewhere, and can be seen all around the world, not least in the ecological and social disintegration one can see perhaps most vividly in the devastation of America's great urban areas. One need not catalogue here the species lost, the weather patterns disrupted, the changes evident. Each year, scientists record newly recognized consequences of our technological juggernaut society for the natural world; each year we see new signs of how a society fragments and collapses when it no longer recognizes a sacred centre.

But nature is resilient, and the archetypes that it reflects do not change, nor does their spiritual origin. Reflecting this profound resilience of nature, and these perennial archetypes that nature itself reflects, Native American traditions remain remarkably vital in the face of such changes as modernity has wrought. As we have seen, Native American cultures affirm primordial values and sacred truths that do not change over time, regardless of particular cultural situations. Because these values and truths are primordial – like the symbol of the cross in the circle – they can be carried on, rediscovered, and applied anew, time and again.

Above all, the American Indian traditions reflect a unified understanding of nature,

BELOW *A Hopi Indian performs a traditional Buffalo Dance.*

religion, culture, art, and ways of living. As Joseph Epes Brown has pointed out, 'art' or 'religion' are not seen as separate categories in tribal cultures. Rather, 'art' is manifested in ritual and in objects used in daily life, in clothing and implements. What is more, the designs used in these forms reflect the archetypes found in nature, and are central to traditional native religion. Nature, the landscape, the cultural traditions are all interwoven and inseparable, part of an integrated spiritual way of life that reflects its archetypal and primordial centre.

This integration has much to tell us in the modern world. Certainly, it speaks to us of openness to the 'other world' seen in visions and in the afterlife. For this is fundamental to all the American Indian traditions, despite their many external differences: nature, culture, ritual, the landscape, all are informed by and reflect the visionary world. Indeed, the Sioux, Lame Deer said: 'I think that when it comes right down to it, all the Indian religions are all somehow part of the same belief, the same mystery'.[74] These traditions, in their affirmation of this essential mystery of life and its relation to the spiritual realm, at the very least reaffirm our own primordial meaning and significance.

Many tribal people object to attempts at absorbing Indian traditions into other religions, or to various 'new age' efforts of white people to 'become Indian' in superficial ways through weekend workshops and the like.[75] One need not advocate such things, however, in order to recognize that these attempts to assimilate some aspects of Indian tradition into modern life reflect a lack of tradition in these modern peoples' lives, and in a way affirm the perennial, enduring significance of what the Native American traditions truly embody.

At heart, then, Native American traditions represent, as Paul Radin noted, not the results of some 'evolutionary process', but the embodiment of primordial, archetypal spiritual truths. One need not romantically view every aspect of all native cultures as ideal and pristine – certainly some indigenous American cultures were violent and cruel in

Two tribes come to peace at last when James Cox (left) Tribal Chairman of the Comanche and Eddie Box (right) Medicine Man of the Southern Ute performed a peace dance and signed a peace treaty on 23 July 1977.

the extreme – but nonetheless, in essence, these cultures do affirm archetypal truths that call to us today because they are beyond historical context. Their myths, their symbols, their ways of life, affirm to us in the modern world something of what it means to be truly human and alive on this earth.

Despite the many crises we face today, few would advocate that modern people should try to return to an aboriginal way of life. In the face of various catastrophes, though, it may well be that only those people capable of carrying on in that way of life will survive. In any event, the Native American traditions represent an important and rich part of our human inheritance, and remind us in an ever more technological and hectic world of what it really means to stand beneath heaven's vault and upon earth's circle: around us the four directions, the waters, the rocks, the birds, the animals, and the winds, and above us the sun or the stars.

We end with the words of Thomas Yellowtail:

Only God knows when the end of this world will come, and when and how it comes will certainly depend on sincere prayers that are offered to Him in the correct way. Each man will pass from this earth in his own time. Some of the prophecies talk only about the end of time; others speak about the break-up of the modern world ... and a return to the traditional ways of our ancestors. I can't say what will happen and whether we will find the spiritual ways of our ancestors in this world or another, but I do know that in either case we still have to make a choice; each one of us most choose at this present moment which path to follow. Each person's prayers can help everyone. The person who prays and remembers God will receive the greatest benefit for himself and for others.[76]

THE
ELEMENT
LIBRARY
NATIVE
AMERICAN
TRADITIONS

BIBLIOGRAPHY

1. See Knud Rasmussen, *Intellectual Culture of the Iglulik Eskimos,* Vol. VII.1, *Report of the Fifth Thule Expedition,* 1921-1924, Nordisk Ferlag, 1929.

2. Black Elk, *The Sacred Pipe,* J.E. Brown, ed., Penguin USA, 1972, p. 9.

3. More than one traditional tribal elder early in the twentieth century, when shown a photograph of a bomb and told what it entails, turned away in incredulity that men would war in such a way.

4. J. Neihardt, ed., *Black Elk Speaks,* Pocket, 1972, p.226.

5. Michael Oren Fitzgerald, ed., *Yellowtail, Crow Medicine Man and Sun Dance Chief,* University of Oklahoma Press, 1992, p. 74.

6. ibid., p. 75.

7. See Stevenson, M. Coxe, 'The Zuni Indians', *The Annual Report of the Bureau of American Ethnology, 23,* 1904, pp. 579 ff.

8. Joseph Epes Brown, ed., *The Sacred Pipe, Black Elk's Account of the Seven Rites of the Oglala Sioux,* Penguin USA, 1971, p. 6.

9. *Yellowtail,* op. cit., pp. 46-8.

10. ibid., p. 108.

11. The same is true in Tibetan and other cultures with sacred mask dances. Tribes all across the Americas practised mask dances.

12. *Black Elk Speaks,* op. cit., p. 36.

13. *Yellowtail,* p. 48.

14. See on this practice of 'lamenting', Black Elk, *The Sacred Pipe,* op. cit., pp. 44 ff. See also Versluis, *Sacred Earth: The Spiritual Landscape of Native America,* Inner Traditions, 1992, pp. 129 ff.

15. See Arthur Versluis, *Sacred Earth: The Spiritual Landscape of Native America,* Inner Traditions, 1992, pp. 139-44.

16. Frank Waters, *The Book of the Hopi,* Penguin USA, 1963, p. 166.

17. ibid., p. 172.

18. Wallace Black Elk and William Lyon, *Black Elk, The Sacred Ways of a Lakota,* Harper, 1990, pp. 173-5.

19. See Ake Hultkranz, *The Religions of The American Indians,* University of California Press, 1979, pp. 200-201.

20. Here, and throughout the work, the word 'astrology' is used rather than 'astronomy' because the former word, despite its sometimes vulgar manifestations in the modern era, has come to signify study of the stars and planets as regards their significances for the soul, while the latter word has come to mean merely the quantitative analysis of celestial phenomena. Tribal peoples respect and are informed by the former, not the latter.

21. Black Elk, *The Sacred Pipe,* op. cit., pp. 31-2.

22. *Yellowtail,* op. cit., p. 165.

23. ibid.

24. *Yellowtail,* op. cit., p. 188.

25. For a discussion of traditional cosmology generally, see Versluis, *Song of the Cosmos: An Introduction to Traditional Cosmology,* Prism Press, 1991.

26. See Mircea Eliade, *Shamanism: Archaic Techniques of Ecstasy,* Princeton University Press, 1971, p. 288.

27. See Chapter I.

28. The neutrality of magic inasmuch as it can be used for good or for ill – and how white magic is affiliated to a traditional religion – is discussed in Versluis, *The Philosophy of Magic,* RKP, 1986.

29. Eliade, op. cit., pp. 321-2.

30. ibid., pp. 324-5.

31. Hultkranz, *Religions,* op. cit., p. 69.

32. Black Elk, *The Sacred Pipe,* op. cit., p. 44.

33. ibid., Ch. IV, pp. 44 ff.

34. See Versluis, *Sacred Earth,* op. cit., on the meeting of native and Christian mysticism, pp. 119 ff.

35. For more on these sites, see Versluis, *Sacred Earth,* op. cit., pp. 48 ff.

36. See John Eddy, 'Archaeoastronomy of North America: Caves, Mounds, Medicine Wheels', in E. Krupp, ed., *In Search of Ancient Astronomies,* McGraw-Hill, 1978, pp. 133 ff.

37. The opinion of some that such sites were created as works of 'abstract art', with no cultural or celestial significance, expresses as clearly as possible the bankruptcy of such interpreters.

38. See Versluis, *Sacred Earth,* op. cit., pp. 67 ff.

39. David Carrasco, *Religions of Mesoamerica,* Harper, 1990, p. 116.

50. Henry Corbin, *Spiritual Body and Celestial Earth: From Mazdaean Iran to Shi'ite Iran,* N. Pearson, trs., Princeton University Press, 1977, p. 12.

51. Joseph Epes Brown, *The Spiritual Legacy of the American Indian,* Crossroad, 1987, p. 46.

52. John Fire and Richard Erdoes, *Lame Deer – Seeker of Visions,* Simon & Schuster, 1972, p. 156.

53. *Lame Deer*, op. cit., p. 239.

54. T. Mails, *Fools Crow*, Doubleday, 1979, p. 160.

55. *Fools Crow*, op. cit., p. 120.

56. *Black Elk Speaks*, Simon and Schuster, 1972, p. 40.

57. ibid., p. 26.

58. ibid.

59. ibid., p. 35.

60. ibid.

61. ibid., pp. 22 and 36.

62. ibid., p. 36.

63. ibid., p. 41.

64. ibid., p. 41.

65. These traditional visionary narratives by religious leaders like Black Elk must be distinguished from novels like those of Carlos Castaneda, who offers forays into the psychic realm of sorcery or witchcraft, or like those of Lynn Andrews, whose fiction and workshops were listed in the American Indian publication *Akwesasne Notes* as characteristic of a growing number of 'new age' 'plastic' medicine men and women.

56. Philip Sherrard, *The Sacred in Life and Art,* Golgonooza Press, 1990, p. 33.

57. *Yellowtail,* op. cit., p. 188.

58. Waters, *Book of the Hopi,* op. cit., p. 204.

59. See Hultkranz, *Native Religions of North America,* Harper & Row, 1987, p. 116.

60. Gene Weltfish, *The Lost Universe: Pawnee Life and Culture,* Basic, 1965, pp. 322-4.

61. Quoted by Joseph Epes Brown, *The Spiritual Legacy of the American Indian,* Crossroad, 1987, p. 84.

62. Weltfish, *Lost Universe,* op. cit., pp. 328-29.

63. Eliade, *Patterns in Comparative Religion,* Meridian, 1963, p. 396.

64. We might add that the Wolf Star is directly connected to and presides over the Pawnee practice, ended in the early nineteenth century, of sacrificing a virgin girl.

65. See Versluis, *Theosophia: Christian Visionary Spirituality,* forthcoming for an extensive discussion of Christian theosophic opponents of materialism and scientism, including such writers as Franz von Baader and Franz Josef Molitor, as well as American 'radical pietists'.

66. See Black Elk, *The Sacred Pipe,* op. cit., pp. 6, 9.

67. *A Basic Call to Consciousness: The Hau de no sau nee Address to the Western World,* Mohawk Nation: Akwasasne Notes, 1978, pp. 9-10.

68. *Yellowtail*, op. cit., p. 150.

69. *Black Elk,* The Sacred Pipe, p. 7.

70. *Yellowtail,* op. cit., pp. 195-6; see Waters, *Book of the Hopi,* op. cit., p. 333.

71. *Yellowtail*, op. cit., p. 187.

72. *Black Elk Speaks*, op. cit., p. 230.

73. For an extremely detailed account of the massacre at Wounded Knee, see Dee Brown, *Bury My Heart at Wounded Knee,* Bantam, 1972.

74. Lame Deer and Richard Erdoes, *Lame Deer, Seeker of Visions,* Simon and Schuster, 1972, p.246.

75. See Note 55.

76. *Yellowtail*, P. 197.

THE
ELEMENT
LIBRARY
NATIVE
AMERICAN
TRADITIONS

GLOSSARY

ACBADADEA Crow word for 'God', Corresponds to the Lakota word *Wakan-Tanka*, often translated as 'Great Spirit'.

ALGONQUIN The language group of tribes such as the Ojibway, Chippewa, and Ottawa whose traditional land is near the Great Lakes region.

ANGAKUK Eskimo term for shaman.

COSMIC REJUVENATION or WORLD RENEWAL Ceremonies central to many Native American traditions, in which the renewal of cosmic forces is celebrated as part of the seasonal or temporal cycles. Cosmic rejuvenation was very important for Aztec and other southern cultures, but is found in various forms across the Americas.

COSMOLOGY Traditional doctrines regarding the cosmos, including the physical, subtle (or psychic), and spiritual realms.

EMERGENCE Myths – including Hopi – according to which people emerged from a dying world into another new world. Emergence myths refer to traditional time cycles. (See **WORLDS**.)

ESOTERIC Adjective used to describe the inward spiritual meaning of a religious symbol, form, ritual or tradition.

GHOST DANCE A pan-Indian shamanic, millennialist and messianic movement that swept many tribes during the late nineteenth century.

HAU DE NO SAU NEE Traditional name of the Six Nations of the Iroquois Confederacy, including such tribes as the Mohawk, the Seneca, the Cayuga, the Onondaga, and the Oneida.

HIEROHISTORY Mythological or archetypal history, which 'happens' before or above time, and which gives meaning to the present. Mythological events happen in hierohistory, and often explain tribal or ritual origins or ancestors. *Hiero* means 'holy' or 'sacred'.

HIEROPHANY Spiritual revelation through the form of, or under the guidance of, a spirit being.

INIPI The traditional purification or sweat lodge ceremony of the Sioux.

INITIATION Ritual blessing and entry into the esoteric truths of a religious tradition; conferring of spiritual protection.

JOSSAKID Algonquin term for a shaman, often affiliated with the 'shaking tent' ceremony to which spirits are called and in which they manifest themselves in the sacred lodge through paranormal phenomena.

KACHINA Spirit of the invisible life forces or powers, according to the Hopi.

LAKOTA Language group of the Sioux Plains tribes.

LAMENTING (Lakota: *hanblecheyapi*): the ritual practice, particularly among Plains tribes, of going out to seek a vision in solitude.

MEDICINE MAN Shaman or holy man, healer.

MEDICINE BUNDLE Collection of sacred, symbolic artifacts kept together in a sacred pouch or bundle; they contain the actual presence of spiritual power.

MIDE(OR MIDEWIWIN) The 'great medicine lodge' or initiatory society of the Algonquin tribes near the Great Lakes region, including the Ojibway and the Chippewa. Initiates of the higher levels are regarded as medicine men. There are four levels of initiation. Members learn about herbs, sacred animals, myths, and in the initiation rites ritually 'die' and are reborn.

NAGUAL Mesoamerican term for one's guardian spirit.

ORENDA (Iroquois) A mysterious psychic or subtle force manifesting in various degrees in certain beings or objects. The Algonquin *manitou* and the Siouxan *wakan* imply roughly equivalent ideas, referring essentially to that which is mysterious, holy, possessed of psychic and spiritual force. *Manitou* may also refer to personified spirit beings.

PETROGLYPHS Carved images or symbols in sandstone bluffs that are directionally oriented and embody the signs of certain spirit beings. Said traditionally to change from year to year.

PEYOTE A hallucinogenic cactus used in certain rites of the Native American Church, a pan-Indian movement that the United States Supreme Court – continuing its restrictions on religious freedom in America – recently declared inaccessible to non-Indians.

PUEBLO Agrarian tribal groups of the south-western United States, including the Hopi and the Zuni.

SUN DANCE The central summer dance of the Plains tribes, including the Sioux and the Crow. It takes place around the centre pole, which signifies the centre of the universe.

TERRAGLYPH Image carved into or built upon the earth itself, like the Great Serpent Mound in Ohio, or the Lyons Serpent intaglio in Kansas.

THERIOMORPHIC Having the form of an animal.

THREE REALMS Physical, subtle, and spiritual. The subtle realm is that of the soul, and the spiritual realm is transcendent, eternal. The physical is animated by the subtle, and both are informed by their spiritual origin. A cosmological understanding found, and expressed variously, in Hindu, Buddhist, Plantonic,

Christian, Judaic, Islamic, and Native American traditions.

TIME CYCLES According to Native American traditions, particularly in Mesoamerica and South America, time is cyclic rather than linear. Currently, we are approaching the prophesied end of one time cycle; the Maya recognized time cycles of many thousands, even millions, of years, very much paralleling Hindu and Buddhist traditions.

TOTEM An archetypal animal, such as the otter or the deer, symbolic of a particular clan; traditionally in many tribes it is forbidden to marry someone in the same clan.

WORLDS According to some southern tribes, in particular here the Hopi, human beings have emerged from three previous worlds, each of which collapsed due to catastrophe. According to the Hopi, we are currently in *Tuwaqachi*, the 'Completed' and fourth world. There are said to be five more worlds, for a total of nine. Essentially, 'world' here really refers to 'time cycle'. (See also **THREE REALMS** and **TIME CYCLES**.)

WAKAN-TANKA A Siouxan word, usually defined as 'Great Spirit'. *Wakan* means 'holy, wonderful, mysterious', and *Wakan-Tanka* can be defined as 'Great *Wakan*'.

FURTHER READING

Avaloka: A Journal of Traditional Religion and Culture, Vols. I-VII, 1986-1992. A source for articles on many world religious traditions, including the Native American traditions. Many previously unpublished translations.

A Basic Call to Consciousness: The Hau de no sau nee Address to the Western World, Mohawk Nation: Akwesasne Notes, 1978. An unusual document, harshly critical of modernity.

Black Elk (John G. Neihardt, ed.) *Black Elk Speaks; Being the Life Story of a Holy Man of the Oglala Sioux*. Pocket, 1972. A classic narrative.

Black Elk (Joseph Epes Brown, ed.) *The Sacred Pipe: Black Elk's Account of the Seven Rites of the Oglala Sioux*, Penguin USA, 1971. Another classic account, informed by the editor's knowledge of comparative religion.

Brown, J.E. *The Spiritual Legacy of the American Indian*, Crossroad, 1987. A valuable overview

Carrasco, D. *Religions of Mesoamerica*, Harper, 1990. The best survey on this subject.

Drury, N. *The Elements of Shamanism*, Element Books, 1989. Useful for its discussion of controversial novelists such as Castaneda and Andrews.

Eliade, M. (R. Sheed, trs.) *Patterns in Comparative Religion*, World, 1963. Useful for its thematic treatment.

Eliade, M. *Shamanism: Archaic Techniques of Ecstasy*, Bollingen, 1972. The classic study of this subject.

González, F. *Los Simbolos Precolumbinos: Cosmogonia, Teogonia, Cultura*, Ediciones Obelisco, 1989. A prolific author and editor, González here considers the Precolumbian American religions in light of the world religious traditions and perennial religion.

Guénon, R. (A. MacNab, trs.) *The Symbolism of the Cross*, Lusac,
1975. A classic study by this seminal writer.

Guénon, R. (A. Moore, trs.) *Fundamental Symbols of Sacred Science*, Quinta Essentia, 1992. An important collection of essays on sacred symbolism.

Hultkranz, A. *Native Religions of North America: The Power of Visions and Fertility*, Harper & Row, 1987. A small book focusing primarily on the Shoshoni and the Zuni.

Hultkrantz, A. (M. Setterwall, trs.) *The Religions of the American Indians*, University of California Press, 1979. The best of the broad academic surveys.

Lame Deer and Erdoes, R. *Lame Deer, Seeker of Visions*, Simon & Schuster, 1972. Another important book from the Plains Indian tradition, of the order of *Black Elk Speaks*.

Lyon, W. S. and Wallace Black Elk, *Black Elk: The Sacred Ways of a Lakota*, Harper & Row, 1990. An interesting view of a shaman's work in the modern world.

Mails, T. E. *Fools Crow*, Doubleday, 1979. A remarkable and prophetic book.

Mavor, J. and Dix, B. *Manitou: The Sacred Landscape of New England's Native Civilization*, Inner Traditions, 1989. A fascinating study of New England sacred sites, and of the relations between whites and Indians. Revision of history at its best.

Michell, J. and Rhone, C. *Twelve-tribe Nations and the Science of Enchanting the Landscape*, Phanes, 1991. An enchanting and provocative book, especially for those interested in comparing traditional Christian and Native American views of sacred landscape.

Sherrard, P. *The Sacred in Life and Art*, Golgonooza Press, 1990. A very important, beautifully written and provocative book, not yet widely known.

THE
ELEMENT
LIBRARY
NATIVE
AMERICAN
TRADITIONS

Tedlock, D. and B. (eds.) *Teachings from the American Earth: Indian Religion and Philosophy*, Liveright, 1975. A very good anthology, including many important writings from authors like Radin and Walker.

Tooker, E. (ed.) *Native North American Spirituality of the Eastern Woodlands, Sacred Myths, Dreams, Visions, Speeches, Healing Formulas, Rituals, and Ceremonials*, Paulist Press, 1979. A fine anthology of Native eastern woodlands mythological and ceremonial traditions.

Vaillant, G. C. *Aztecs of Mexico*, Pelican, 1965. A useful academic overview.

Versluis, A. *Sacred Earth: The Spiritual Landscape of Native America*, Inner Traditions, 1992. An extensive study, informed by comparison to other world religions, of Native American understanding of landscape and sacred sites.

Versluis, A. *Song of the Cosmos: An Introduction to Traditional Cosmology*, Prism Press, 1991. As the subtitle suggests, an introduction to traditional cosmology drawing on the world religions.

Walker, J.J. (R. J. DeMallie, ed.) *Lakota Belief and Ritual*, University of Nebraska Press, 1980. Newly edited collection of interviews with traditional Lakota Sioux of the nineteenth century.

Waters, F. *The Book of the Hopi*, Penguin USA, 1963. The best overview of Hopi mythology and culture.

Weltfish, G. *The Lost Universe: Pawnee Life and Culture*, University of Nebraska Press, 1965. Excellent reconstruction of Pawnee culture during the nineteenth century.

Wissler, C. *Indians of the United States*, Doubleday, 1966. Originally published in 1940, still an important and sympathetic study.

Yellowtail, T. and Fitzgerald M. O. *Yellowtail: Crow Medicine Man and Sun Dance Chief, An Autobiography*, University of Oklahoma Press, 1991. A classic autobiography, with much to say on religion and the modern world. Highly recommended.

ACKNOWLEDGEMENTS

Amon Carter Museum 51

Bureau of Ethnology, Smithsonian Institute 13b, 39b, 82

Cameron Collection 14l, 16t, 71, 72

E.T. Archives:
BRITISH MUSEUM 23b;
NATIONAL MUSEUM OF ANTHROPOLOGY, MEXICO 24t;MUSEUM OF MANKIND 22t

Fine Art Photographic Library 15, 16t

Fortean Picture Library 83b;
KLAUS AARSLEFF 8, 23t, 55t, 65; LOREN COLEMAN 64b;
DR ELMAR R.GRUBER 20–1, 24b, 37, 52b, 55b, 66, 67;
DENNIS STACY 64t

The Mansell Collection 44, 46, 63r, 69

Mary Evans Picture Library
17t, 25t, 25b, 30, 34, 39t, 40, 50, 63l

Michael Holdford Photograph 73;
ANDRE BRETON COLLECTION 13t, 49;
BRITISH MUSEUM 11t;
SENOR MUJICA GALLO COLLECTION 26, 42t;
HORNIMAN MUSEUM 74t

Milwaukee Public Museum 54t

Museum of American Indian 14r

Peter Newark's Western Americana
6–7, 9, 12, 16b, 17b, 18r, 19b, 20, 27, 28, 29t, 31t, 32, 33, 36, 38, 42b, 43, 45b, 47, 58, 59, 60, 68, 74b, 75t, 75bl, 76l, 76r, 80

Public Archives of Canada 10, 75br

Range/ Bettman 6l, 45t, 53 54b, 56, 62, 77, 78;
RANGE/ BETTMAN/ UPI 86, 88, 89

Ross County, Ohio Department Board 61

US Bureau of Indian Affairs 83t

INDEX

THE
ELEMENT
LIBRARY
NATIVE
AMERICAN
TRADITIONS